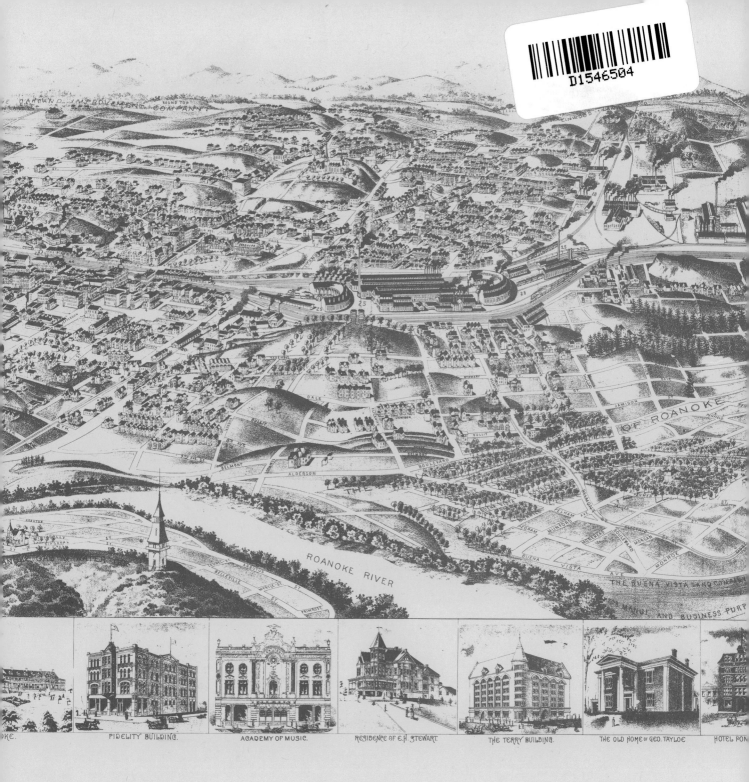

FIDELITY BUILDING. ACADEMY OF MUSIC. RESIDENCE OF E.H. STEWART. THE TERRY BUILDING. THE OLD HOME OF GEO. TAYLOE HOTEL PON

CITY OF
E, VA.

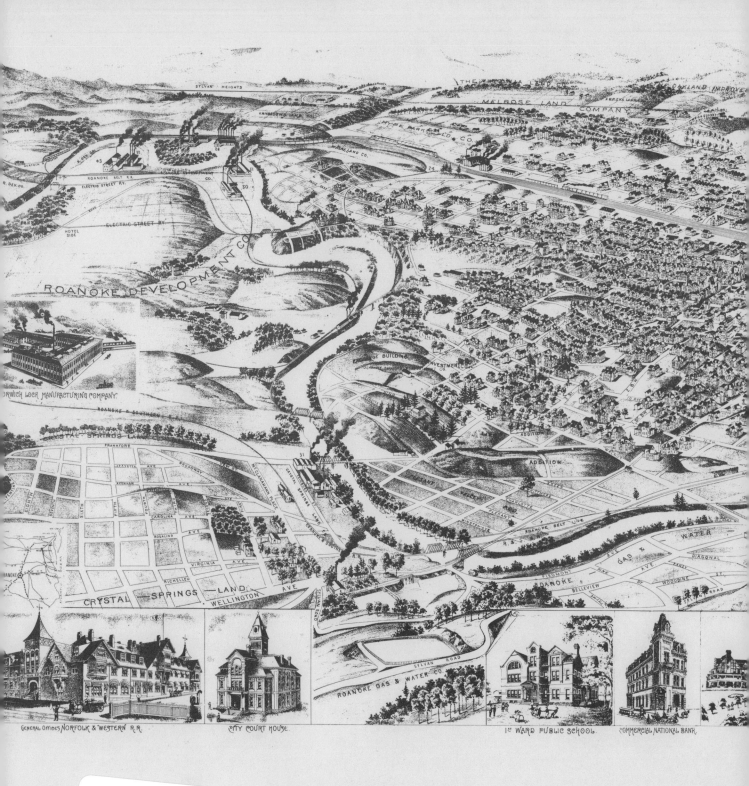

General Offices NORFOLK & WESTERN R.R.   CITY COURT HOUSE.   1ST WARD PUBLIC SCHOOL.   COMMERCIAL NATIONAL BANK.

PERSPECTI

ROAN

The Architectural Heritage
of the Roanoke Valley

The Architectural Heritage
of the
Roanoke Valley

W. L. Whitwell

Lee W. Winborne

Selected Photographs by Judith Farb

University Press of Virginia

Charlottesville

THE UNIVERSITY PRESS OF VIRGINIA
Copyright © 1982 by the Rector and Visitors
of the University of Virginia

First published 1982

Library of Congress Cataloging in Publication Data

Whitwell, W. L. (William Livingston), 1936–
  The architectural heritage of the Roanoke
Valley.

  Bibliography : p.
  Includes index.
  1. Architecture—Roanoke Valley (Va.)
I. Winborne, Lee W.   II. Title.
NA730.V82R68   720′.9756′1   81–12987
ISBN 0–8139–0905–8   AACR2

Printed in the United States of America

Contents

The Roanoke Valley is *home* to many kinds of people with heritages as varied as the streams that trickle down the Blue Ridge Mountains. And the resulting rich variety of architectural forms and styles are what you will discover in the chapters of our book. You won't find Scarlett O'Hara plantation mansions, but rather, homes and buildings that portray a simple life.

Perhaps it is because of the dearth of enormous, ornate mansions that a study of Roanoke Valley architecture had never been done. But it was precisely such neglect—the lack of attention and appreciation of what we have in our part of Virginia—that spurred us on to five years of researching and writing an architectural history.

At the onset we resolved to examine the gamut of valley building and not only the more imposing or high-style edifices. The ordinary buildings, so essential to our study, reveal what the people and their lives were really like in bygone eras. We prefaced our research with one encompassing question: What is here? You will find, as we did, that our architectural heritage in Southwest Virginia is consistently fascinating.

In order to adhere to the strictly scholarly intent of our study, we had to give up all assumptions, hearsay, and oral accounts of family traditions. We believed nothing until we verified it! History already suffers too much from legends and genealogies, which are not always germane to an architectural study anyway.

In the past some social historians have treated Roanoke overgenerously. We painstakingly avoided glamorizing Roanoke in our architectural history. Our region must be seen for what it was, a homey place to live. Only then will our local history fall into place, and its true meaning can begin to be realized.

Although Roanoke is our home and has assimilated us in the combined forty years that we've lived here, we are outsiders in the sense that neither we nor our forefathers were born in the valley. For this reason, we believed we could trace Roanoke's architectural legacy more objectively and with a keener perspective than a native-born person.

Besides the arduous task of sorting fact from fiction in our data, we faced an equal challenge of choosing key structures that represented the historical development of Roanoke architecture, spanning 150 years from when the Scotch-Irish and German pioneers settled here to the shopping-center era of the 1970s. We drove mile after mile sightseeing. Our respite from canvassing the valley's three-hundred square miles during those three and a half years was spent in poring over tax, deed, will, land, inventory, and appraisal books—many of the courthouses' early records had never even been used for historical research before. When we faced a dead-end, old telephone books, surprisingly our most indispensable research tool, often exposed the missing link.

The valley's buildings parallel much of America's architectural history. You will see almost every major nineteenth- and twentieth-century style. In each account of the residences, churches, barns, and commercial establishments we finally selected, you will learn first about the style, then about the method of building, the builder, and any novel or unusual features of the structure. Companion photographs, along with a short treatment of forms similar to the prime example, will help you understand the style period more fully. We dealt with post–World War II styles in a briefer overview because we are not far enough removed in time to know their real significances.

Your greatest pleasure may be (as ours was) in stumbling across new discoveries. The log springhouse illustrated in this book—acknowledged by a leading expert on folk forms to be one of a kind—displays a quaintness that you find especially with the homespun character of log cabins. Several sturdy cabins and other vernacular structures from the pioneer days survive in the valley; you will not want to miss tracking them down. You'll also encounter other valuable finds, such as the Dunkard church left unchanged since the nineteenth century and the 1852–86 journal of an important local builder to which we often refer.

Our survey does not include any building that has been severely altered or torn down, nor does it contain an example merely because someone suggested it was a *must*. We made the decisions ourselves, seeking variety and what exemplified major styles in the valley. We based our selections on the merits of form, detail, and style, with no regard for social or sectional preferences. Some buildings do not reflect a landmark style but stand alone due to their uniqueness.

A map is provided on pp. xiv–xv to assist the reader in locating the structures illustrated. This map, however, offers the reader only a general idea of the location of the buildings illustrated in this book. To visit a specific building, please use this map in conjunction with maps published by the Virginia Department of Highways and Transportation and by each municipality in the Roanoke Valley. You will find some buildings by the grid on our map; others are listed by titled sections that are shaded on the map. Of course, old views and pictures, details, and diagrams are not located on the map.

Geography, history, economics, and politics, although not the focus of our study, are mentioned in relationship to their effects on our architecture. We deliberately left out personal histories unless they directly involved architecture. Because many of the buildings are privately owned and are not open to the public and because owners change, we do not record names of the deed holders. Only in special cases do we describe interiors, as they undergo constant alteration.

We've designed our survey for several levels of reading: You can peruse the over two-hundred photographs for a visual awakening of what's around you, you can glean the basic information by caption skimming, or you can delve into the deeper intricacies of Roanoke's architectural legacy by studying the copy. Whichever method you choose, we expect many of you to carry the book along in your shuttles about the valley and to take personal delight in identifying what you see. Sometimes you may need to refer to the dictionary, because we used architectural terms in order to provide accurate descriptions.

When people move to any new area, the buildings around them influence their first impressions. Innately fascinating, buildings project the accomplishments, desires, values, and limitations of their predecessors. They do not move around as people do, so as long as they stand, they remind us of the past.

And so it is with the buildings here. The Roanoke Valley—crossroads of Southwest Virginia and a microcosm of the later mid-nineteenth century because of its architectural lag—has always shunned trendiness. Its conservative nature is not necessarily bad, however, and the valley offers plenty of buildings interesting in their own right. We hope our study will prompt you to look around your home and see what's there. Our heritage is worth considering. And it's definitely worth preserving. It gives us a sense of identity.

The Architectural Heritage
of the Roanoke Valley

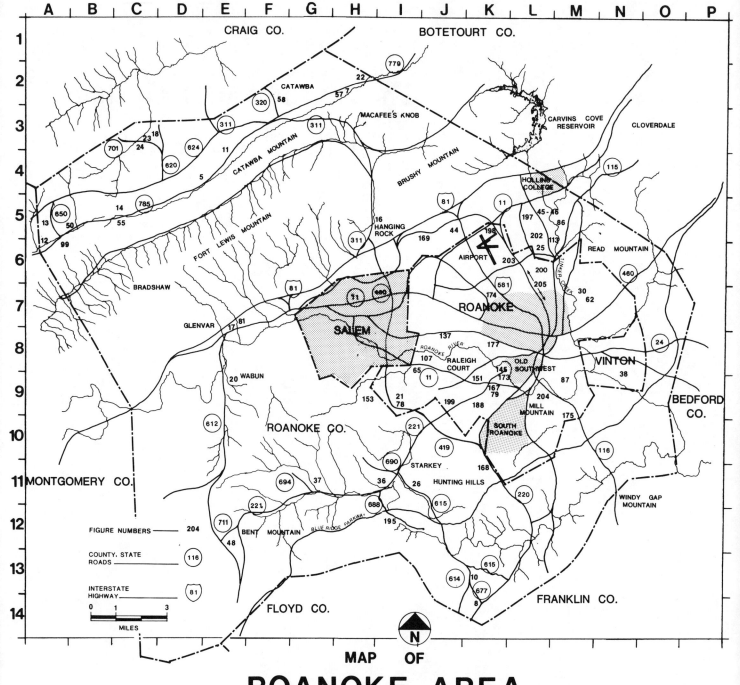

MAP OF

ROANOKE AREA

5	Rectangular Log Cabin	D4		18	Overhang Outbuilding	D3
7	Rectangular Log Cabin	H2		20	Overhang Outbuilding	E9
8	Square Log Cabin	K14		21	Overhang Outbuilding	I 9
10	Single-Crib Barn	K13		22	Overhang Outbuilding	H2
11	Single-Crib Barn	E3		23	Overhang Outbuilding	C3
12	Single-Crib Barn	A6		24	Tobacco Barn	C3
13	Double-Crib Barn	A5		25	Stone House (with brick addition)	L6
14	Double-Crib Barn	C5		26	I-Form House (Speedwell)	I 11
15	Forebay Bank Barn	Salem		30	I-Form House (Belmont)	M7
16	Bake Oven	I 5		32	I-Form House	Salem
17	Overhang Outbuilding	E7		33	I-Form House	Salem

Introduction

Mountains surround the Roanoke Valley of Virginia. It's a beautiful place. But the same mountains that contribute to its sheer natural beauty also bequeath to the valley a relative isolation and, subsequently, a limited economy. Herein lie clues to the valley's simplicity of architecture.

The valley fans the southern terminus of the Shenandoah Valley, sometimes called the Great Valley of Virginia, which runs north and south between the Blue Ridge Mountains on the east and the Allegheny Mountains on the west. Geographically, the Roanoke Valley lies between parallels 37° 7′ and 37° 25′ and between meridians 79° 50′ and 80° 16′.[1] Clockwise from its extreme southern boundary point, the area is surrounded by Montgomery, Craig, Botetourt, Bedford, Franklin, and Floyd counties.

The legally constituted municipalities of Roanoke County, the city of Roanoke, the city of Salem, and the town of Vinton comprise the Roanoke Valley. For the purpose of this architectural survey, the term *Roanoke Valley* will mean the entire area, which covers nearly three-hundred square miles.[2]

Three main units make up the valley's physical setting: the Blue Ridge

Mountain area in the southeastern part, the Fort Lewis–Brushy Mountain–Catawba Valley complex in the northwestern part, and the Roanoke Valley itself, which is broad and flat, in the central and eastern parts. Approximately half of the whole area is mountainous, with elevations ranging from 880 feet to 3960 feet above sea level.[3] Most boundaries fall upon the crests of these mountain ridges.

Springs abound, several with an unusually large flow. Numerous sinks and caves with underground water circulation make inroads into the soluble limestone commonly found in the area. Several large streams meander through the valley. With headwaters to the west, the Roanoke River bisects the county from west to east on its way to North Carolina. All of the valleys south of Catawba Mountain drain into the Roanoke River, which cuts through the Blue Ridge at the eastern extremity of Roanoke County. The area north of Catawba Mountain is drained by Catawba Creek, a tributary of the James River. The northwestern portion of the Catawba Valley drains via the North Fork into the Roanoke River. Indeed, settlers were drawn to the area by the water and the arable, well-drained soil.

Despite much settlement in the twentieth century, approximately three-fifths of the whole area remains wooded. The southeastern portion still consists of heavily forested mountains with narrow, steep ravines and valleys. In the northwest are long, thin parallel valleys and mountains with dense forests on the ridges, drained by small streams.[4] Because of its mild climate and considerable precipitation, the valley always has been notably lush. Stands of deciduous and evergreen trees cling to the mountainsides, and thick pastures dot the valley. Although the climate is basically temperate, summers can be hot and humid and winters cold with occasionally heavy snowfalls.

Geologically, the Roanoke Valley is formed by ridges on outcrops of resistant rock above lowlands eroded along belts of less-resistant rock. The less-resistant rock, technically a pre-Cambrian crystalline rock, weathers readily and produces a heavy red soil.[5] Because of the soil's high clay content, brick has been a prevalent building material.

The physical setting of the valley, its natural attributes, and even the weather all influenced the kinds of structures that were built here, as well as how and where they were placed on the land. History left its mark on the architecture too. Three major periods distinguish the historical development of the valley: the pioneer days in the late eighteenth and early nineteenth centuries; subsequent steady growth through the nineteenth century; and the coming of the railroad in the late nineteenth century, which triggered a population explosion and the start of twentieth-century metropolitan Roanoke.

1

Big Lick in 1853
Virginia Sketchbook, 1853, by Lewis Miller, p. 25. An early view of Big Lick, which was to become Roanoke City, was drawn by Lewis Miller (1796–1882) in 1853. This relatively unknown artist, who was also a carpenter and world traveler, left a record of everyday life scenes, which he viewed in his wanderings. Best known to Pennsylvania-German scholars for his chronicles of York, Pennsylvania, Miller made a number of drawings in southwest Virginia as he passed through the area. In simple, freely drawn lines with a strange sense of scale, he represented what he saw with great accuracy. As a carpenter, he would have understood buildings, so his sketches are doubtlessly correct. In a small notebook (9¾ inches by 7¼ inches), Lewis Miller's drawings provide a visual history and a wealth of pictorial detail.

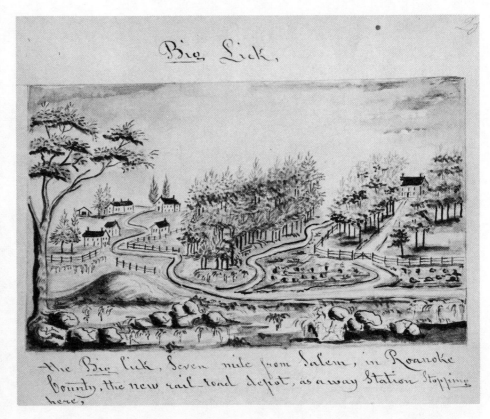

Big Lick,

The Big Lick, Seven mile from Salem, in Roanoke County, the new rail road depot, as a way Station Stopping here,

Unfortunately, there is little reliable information for the pioneer period. Genealogists, the Works Progress Administration in 1942, and other historians have written accounts full of errors, but a comprehensive, scholarly study on the Valley's earliest settlement has yet to be done.

What is known is that the Roanoke Valley began as a crossroads for animals, then for the Indians, and later for the explorers and settlers. From prehistoric times, animals were attracted to the Valley's salt licks, created by the salty waters from various small springs retained in ponds. The area became known as Big Lick and was called by that name on many colonial maps. In April 1746, Augusta County—which took in Roanoke prior to the formation of Botetourt County (November 1769) and its inclusion of the Roanoke Valley—certified Erwin Patterson as constable "near the Great Lick."[6] Travelers through the area in 1753 also noted the large buffalo lick, where many animals congregated because the swamp contained salt.[7]

2

Big Lick in the Mid-Nineteenth Century

This picture overlooks the area that has since developed into Roanoke City. The Valley may be recognized by Fort Lewis Mountain on the left, McAfee's Knob in the center, Tinker Ridge to the right, and Round Hill at the far right in front of Tinker Ridge. Unfortunately, all the buildings seen here are gone, and none can now be identified with certainty.

Following various trails and primitive roads, as well as the Catawba Creek and Roanoke River, tradesmen, explorers, and settlers had reached the area around 1730. The pioneers moved down the Great Valley from eastern Pennsylvania along the so-called Great Road, or Valley Pike, from Carlisle, Pennsylvania, to Bristol, Tennessee, on approximately the same path that Route 11 follows today. Southwest Virginia was settled primarily by these Scotch-Irish and Pennsylvania Germans, with only a few English settlers crossing the mountains from Tidewater Virginia.

The Pennsylvania Germans in particular searched for rich farmland. And they found it. The plentiful hardwood trees indicated fertile soil with limestone below. Bold springs, good soil, and abundant pasture were ideal for the establishment of small independent farms. These livestock and crop farms, some of which exist today, eventually made the settlers prosperous.[8]

The journals kept by Moravian missionaries in 1749 as they journeyed from Bethlehem, Pennsylvania, to the New River in Southwest Virginia and back provide some of the best, earliest sources for understanding the primitive architecture of the settlers.[9] A journal entry states that one eve-

ning in the Shenandoah Valley the Moravians lodged in an "English cabin." After swimming across the James River, they came to what must have been a poor home, for they commented: "we had to lie on bear skins around the fire like the rest. The manner of living is rather poor in this district" (probably the northern part of Botetourt County today). On November 17, 1749, they crossed Catawba Creek and stayed with a miller "as there was no house for twelve miles." The next day, after a heavy snow, they crossed Catawba Creek again and afterwards a branch of the Roanoke, the North Fork, some thirty times. Later that day they reported that "the Lord helped us . . . and brought us in the evening to an English house where we enjoyed the comfort of a good fire." After reaching the New River, they turned around for the return journey to Bethlehem, and on November 28 they again passed the Catawba and a winding branch of the Roanoke "about thirty times,"[10] but they made no mention of any houses. In October 1753 another group of Moravians traveled through the Roanoke Valley from Bethlehem to what is now Winston-Salem, North Carolina. This group stayed in tents while in the Roanoke area; unfortunately, they did not comment on any architecture.[11]

3
Roanoke in the Twentieth Century
From nine stories above the city of Roanoke, the same outline of the mountains as in the early photograph of Big Lick (fig. 2) may be seen. The Roanoke Valley has developed into a thriving metropolitan area since the nineteenth century.

5

By 1753, roads and mills were being built, as recorded in court orders in Augusta County. Between 1747 and 1767, in a variety of transactions, 1600 acres (more or less), on which some of Roanoke City is located today, were granted to Thomas and Tasker Tosh.[12] During this period and throughout the eighteenth century, land grants were given to individuals.[13] A grant, or patent, was a legal process by which a tract of land was conveyed to someone by the king of England after a surveyor's report had been made, the governor of the colony had attended a session of the executive council, and the grant had been noted in a patent book. The English kings did not prepare these papers, but their royal seals were attached.[14]

King George III, who reigned from 1760 to 1820, used a map called the Red Line Map in negotiations for peace after the American Revolution. Prepared in 1755 by surveyor John Mitchell, this map showed only Catawba Creek in what is today Roanoke County.[15] This mention makes clear the importance of the Catawba area during early settlement and may indicate that it was the first section settled. Some of the valley's oldest existing houses and cabins are there.

After the War of 1812, a navigation company attempted to make the Roanoke River navigable from Weldon, North Carolina, to Salem, Virginia, but the plan never worked. A canal system on the James River that was extended westward to Buchanan and improved roads made the Roanoke area more accessible, however.

While prolonged Indian warfare and many hardships characterized the pioneer period, steady growth and prosperous farming delineated the years from 1783 to 1882. The towns of Salem and Big Lick came into being, and Roanoke County was formed.

As the crossroads for a number of turnpikes, the village of Salem developed earlier than Big Lick (later Roanoke City). Salem was surveyed in 1802 and was laid out into blocks for potential buyers. On January 6, 1806, the town was established officially by an act of the General Assembly.[16] In 1836, the year of its incorporation, Salem had "70 houses, 6 stores, 3 taverns, 3 churches, 3 schools, 2 mills, 1 tannery, 5 blacksmith shops, and 8 other small businesses, for a population of 350 people."[17] In 1845, Henry Howe described the town as a "neat" village with a population of 450.[18] At that time Salem was the valley's largest community. In the late 1840s and the 1850s, the town developed a number of institutions, including banks, two springs resorts, and a college.

In 1836, a gazetteer noted "Big Lick, P. O." on one of its maps, but made no mention of population, houses, taverns, churches, or anything else.[19] In 1838 Roanoke County was carved from Botetourt.

Inventories between 1838 and 1849 indicate the lack of wealth and the basically rural economy of the area at this time.[20] The 1840 census, reported by Henry Howe, showed increasing prosperity coming to the area: "Much of the soil of the county, particularly on the Roanoke River in the vicinity of Big Lick, is of almost unequaled fertility and productive in hemp, wheat, and tobacco." In 1845, Roanoke County, as again reported by Howe, showed a total population of 5,499. The county produced Indian corn, tobacco, and many other agricultural items.[21] Big Lick, situated in the section that today is Orange Avenue and the Interstate 581 interchange, had one Baptist church and a few houses.

Both Salem and Big Lick were affected by the coming of the railroads, the key to the third major development in the valley's history. In 1852 the Virginia and Tennessee Railroad began laying tracks from Lynchburg to Bristol and passed through Big Lick and Salem. By connecting the Roanoke Valley with Lynchburg—an older, more established town—the rail service gave valley residents easier access to a better marketplace.

The east-west line later merged with the Atlantic, Mississippi, and Ohio Railroad (AM & O). In 1876 the AM & O went broke. Some businessmen from Philadelphia who realized the growing importance coal would have in the nation's future bought into the New River and the Shenandoah Valley railroad companies. In 1881 they purchased the assets of the AM & O to form the Norfolk and Western Railway (N & W). They planned to extend the New River Company into the coal fields and the Shenandoah lines southward to meet the N & W at Big Lick.[22] The railroad owners made the junction site its home office; they made this decision with care—not arbitrarily, as popular opinion has expressed.

This integration of the railway system north to south with lines east to west proved crucial to N & W's long-range success. Today the N & W lines stretch from the coalfields to the ocean, with coal the railway's ongoing profit maker. The development of the railroad shaped the history of Southwest Virginia and the Roanoke Valley in a definite manner.

When N & W officials selected Big Lick for its headquarters in 1882, they foresaw the thousands of jobs the railroad and resulting industry would create. To encourage orderly growth and to provide housing for the influx of workers, they formed the Roanoke Land and Improvement Company. The city of Roanoke was born—and a swampland was transformed into a liveable area. Big Lick, which had been incorporated in 1874, searched for a more dignified name and finally agreed on "Roanoke" in 1882. In 1884 the boom town was incorporated as a city.

During the Civil War, the valley had experienced only a few minor skirmishes, but building had come to a halt as people struggled to survive

4
Salem in 1853
Virginia Sketchbook, 1853, by
Lewis Miller, p. 30. Seen from
the extreme southern end of the
valley, Salem appears as a small
cluster of houses, with two conspicuous church spires. Compare this view with figure 75,
below, which shows Salem from
the north. The ridged quality of
the mountains of this region is
emphatically portrayed.

through difficult times. When peace did return, building started anew.
Salem and Roanoke (still Big Lick then) were small communities. According to William McCauley, Big Lick had "3 churches, 8 stores, 1 bank, 5
tobacco factories, 1 mill, 1 factory, 6 small industries, 2 photograph galleries, and 3 saloons."[23] Another author described Big Lick in more colorful
terms.

> Upon completion of the [railroad] a few settlers'
> houses were scattered about the site of Big Lick and
> on Feb. 28, 1874, the little village was incorporated
> as the town of Big Lick. . . . The little town was de-
> pendent for its support entirely upon the rich sur-
> rounding agricultural region. When this brighter day
> dawned upon this place of destiny, there was nothing
> inviting about the appearance of the easy-going old
> town. Off from the railroad to the north upon the roll-
> ing hills were a few rude buildings. A few wealthy
> farmers of this section had their residences in and
> near the town, but there were no stately mansions of

surpassing elegance. The streets were of the most primitive character, and the business buildings were constructed for actual necessity rather than for convenience or handsome appearance. While the surrounding scenery was attractive, the immediate site of the city, or what was to become the city, was decidedly uninviting. In fact, what is now the business portion of Roanoke was a marshy swamp, and it is said that one early investor decided not to purchase what is now part of the most valuable business property because of the constant croaking of frogs in the swamp.[24]

The year after Roanoke became the site for N & W's headquarters, a *Baltimore Sun* reporter visited the city. Of the new railroad town, he wrote in 1883: "At night with the red-light beacons of barrooms ablaze over the plank sidewalks, and the music of banjos and violins coming through the open windows, the town suggested a mining camp."[25]

In the post–Civil War period the tobacco industry rose to importance. Warehouses for smoking tobacco, chewing tobacco, and snuff, as well as small cigar-manufacturing shops, were built. Most tobacco was grown and cured in Franklin County; only a small amount was raised in the Roanoke area.

In the late nineteenth and early twentieth centuries both Roanoke and Salem underwent great development. Roanoke's population soared from 5,000 in 1884 to 26,000 in 1902.[26] Salem's population also increased, especially after a big promotion in the 1890s, when the Salem Improvement Company advertised some 900 acres of land for development. Street improvements, downtown buildings, iron bridges, and other features were offered as inducements to industry.[27]

After 1900, public utilities, construction, transportation, and trade provided thousands of jobs for valley residents. Today, diversified manufacturing flourishes. The Valley serves as a major trade, financial, industrial, cultural, and transportation center and is actually the largest metropolitan area in Southwest Virginia. The Norfolk and Western Railway—as well as Interstate Route 81, which now traverses Roanoke County from northeast to southwest—enhances its crossroads status. The county remains rural at its boundaries, but the rest of it is rapidly being overwhelmed by metropolitan spread and suburban development.

From the time of the pioneers in 1750 and subsequent steady growth, through the expansion of the railroad, to present-day urban sprawl, the architecture that developed at this valley crossroads reveals much about the past culture.

Using traditional forms, the early settlers established themselves within the natural setting. Folk housing was generally owner-built, and the design reflected the builder's cultural heritage. Settlers did not obtain designs from publications or other outside sources. Only occasionally did they use current styles, and then just for embellishments. Their traditional plans were intuitive or familiar, often remembered from their ancestors. Their tools and building techniques also had been handed down from generation to generation. The same construction techniques and available materials were used for all buildings, no matter what the function. Houses, log cabins, and barns were built exactly the same way. Although the folk houses of the nineteenth-century settlers fell into only a few types, some of their cabins, I houses (basically houses with a room on each side of a central hall), hall-and-parlor houses, and four-over-four room houses still exist.

There were no large plantation houses, however, built in the Roanoke Valley as there were in the Tidewater area of Virginia. Valley housing developed within the context of a small agricultural economy. Farming enterprises merely supported the family; they never reached a commercial scale.

In the first half of the nineteenth century a new architectural style swept America. Monumental, classical forms of the so-called Greek Revival took over, partially as a reaction against the previous aristocratic English style. Classical Greek architecture was rediscovered and was made America's own. Small wooden farmhouses were often disguised as temples. The Greek Revival created large effects on a monumental scale by using nailed-together, machine-sawed parts. This allusion to the ancient world expressed America's newly realized confidence and power. Greek Revival style flowered in the Roanoke Valley until well after the Civil War. The Gothic Revival style, so important to nineteenth-century romanticism, never attained the widespread popularity of the Greek Revival either in the Valley or elsewhere in America.

Other revivals and foreign influences became important about the middle of the nineteenth century. At the time of the Civil War, America looked to Second-Empire France for stylish architecture. The Mansard roof, with its strong verticality and heavy, rich ornament (often described by the term *Victorian*), came into vogue in the 1870s. A hybrid architecture grew out of the nineteenth century; only recently has it become possible to separate the wide variety of romantic styles that were derivative in their sources but creative in floor plan, plumbing, central heating, and kitchen facilities.

Generally, the post–Civil War period architecture is remembered for opulence, which often became ostentatious. When cash crops such as tobacco began to replace subsistence farming in the Roanoke Valley, larger, more pretentious houses were built—still in traditional forms, although up-to-date styles were sometimes used on the exteriors. The Valley's agrarian society was transformed by new technology, increased population, and improved transportation systems. Commerce and industry created new wealth; an urban architectural culture emerged in the valley by the 1890s.

The *Virginia Classified Business Directory* for 1893–94 lists four architectural firms in the Roanoke area and contains two advertisements for companies providing architectural millwork. One advertisement read: "J. B. Pollard & Co., Architects and Builders-Plans and specifications furnished on short notice. Also dealers in sash, blinds, doors, moldings, stair rails, brackets, newels, glass, builder's hardware, iron fences, etc."[28]

At the end of the nineteenth century, advanced construction technology made new types of commercial buildings possible in the growing city of Roanoke. Academically correct classical styles, as well as Renaissance and Baroque models from Europe were featured at the Chicago World's Fair of 1893. As the twentieth century opened, architectural design split into many approaches. The Neocolonial style, which has continued to the present day, was but one of the historically derivative designs that found popularity in the Roanoke Valley. Changing needs led the area to functionalism, with a heritage rooted in modern Europe and America. After World War II, what is today called "modern" architecture began to appear in Roanoke. Commercial buildings were built in accordance with this new approach, as were a few churches and some public buildings.

Roanoke Valley architecture is characterized less by desire to impress or to be fashionable than by complacency. As in the past eight generations, builders, architects, contractors, and speculators tend even today to be conservative. The dominant characteristic of Valley architecture is its lag in adopting current styles; because of its innate conservativism, it retains styles ten to twenty years after they lose popularity nationally. Only buildings with a pure profit motive, such as in the strip developments of the Valley, are truly up-to-date.

The Valley does not spend money on the avant-garde. Its architecture is seldom trendy. Local architects and builders in the past have designed pragmatically functional buildings for their clients. Because most builders follow standardized plans, the twentieth-century architectural firms design for a limited clientele. Consequently, few architects have made their mark on the Valley. The resulting stability and provincialism are not without architectural merit, however; they have produced some art.

The geography of the land and its economics, history, and politics have all played expressive roles in fashioning the architectural heritage of the Roanoke Valley.

A note on dating buildings with the use of circa

1. A quarter-century date (such as c. 1825, c. 1850, c. 1875, c. 1900) means a building may actually be dated sometime within twenty-five years before or twenty-five years after the given date.

2. A date ending in zero or five (such as c. 1840 or c. 1845) suggests closer approximation.

3. A date with *circa* ending in any number except zero or five (such as c. 1876 or c. 1889) means a building may actually be dated by specific evidence sometime within a very few years before or after the given date.

4. A date without *circa* indicates that there is evidence for the specific date assigned.

5
Rectangular Log Cabin
Route 785, Roanoke County: Catawba
c. 1840

The log-cabin tradition calls to mind an image of our ancestors and the history of America, but the log cabin is not an indigenous American form. The true history of log-cabin construction is obscure, but the mythology of the log cabin has become firmly entrenched in the American mind. In the campaigns of Andrew Jackson (1828), Zachary Taylor (1848), and Abraham Lincoln (1860), politicians projected the log-cabin image of democracy and its triumph over the wilderness. The log cabin, the Indian, the long Kentucky rifle, and the coonskin cap were all associated with democracy, frontier spirit, the common man, and all those traits in which Americans like to believe.

The log cabin as an architectural form celebrates the vanished frontier world—a wedge between civilization and the unknown. This form may be

13

read as a document giving information about those settlers who did not leave many written records. This log cabin in Catawba, built on a stone foundation and with simple log construction, is typical of many one-and-a-half story cabins in the valley. The cabin has a gabled roof, a stone chimney, and asymmetrically placed windows. The front entrance opening close to the fireplace is on the long side of the structure. A rear door is directly opposite the front door. Originally there was also another back door in a second room. This simple form of architecture may be seen not only in the Roanoke area but all up and down the Shenandoah Valley.

A simple building was constructed by piling hewn logs one on top of another to make a basic unit, and the corners were joined by a V-notched joint (see fig. 6). V-notching was common in the valley, but half dovetailing, full dovetailing, and saddle notching were occasionally done. Most log cabins were well constructed of hewn, squared logs. The floor joists on the Catawba cabin are notched into the square sill at the front and the rear of the cabin. The square wooden sill, upon which the cabin rests, appears to be a southern characteristic.[1] The builder of a log cabin needed a simple set of tools, particularly a good axe and an adz. Most of the time log cabins were immediately given an outer covering. Shingles were most common in the north, but boards were generally used in Roanoke County. The insides were also covered. Protection from the elements by various layers of insulation was a primary consideration.

In hewn-log construction there were spaces between the logs, so chinking was necessary to make the building weatherproof. In the Roanoke area the spaces were often filled with strips of wood left over from squaring the logs. The strips were forced in at an angle, and they also helped to keep the logs from settling. The smallest spaces were then stuffed with mud, clay, plaster mixed with horsehair, or any other suitable substance. After the logs had been piled as high as desired, poles were laid across to form joists for the loft. To give headroom in the loft area, the walls were continued up about four feet above the loft floor, and then the roof was begun. A gable of simple rafters formed the top. The rafters usually butted onto each other in the German manner.[2] A chimney on a gable end could be of various materials including wood, brick, or stone, as here in Catawba.

The shape of most log cabins in the Valley of Virginia is that of a simple rectangle. An appraisal of a farm in this area in 1754–55 shows a log house ten feet by fifteen feet.[3] This cabin in Catawba, which is twenty-one feet by twenty-eight feet, is larger than many. The front and back doors were normally opposite each other, and at least one window was near the hearth for light, as in this Catawba cabin. Construction with logs in

14

America was Swedish-German in origin, but the shape of a rectangular log cabin was Scotch-Irish. In Ireland and Scotland the same shapes may be seen built of stone. The history of the construction of a cabin of logs has been traced to Bohemia, western Moravia, and Silesia (now north-western Czechoslovakia). In all of these places, log construction similar to the American technique is found.[4] The usual pioneer American cabin is made of hardwood logs hewn flat on two sides. Additions to log cabins—such as sheds, lean-tos, kitchens, front porches, ells, or wings of any kind—were added on as needed. Space specialization was seldom used; expansion was mainly by addition.

Log cabins are traditional forms of material culture representative of man's ability to deal with the environment. These forms are truly folk, traditional, indigenous, and nonacademic. They have been overlooked—indeed, ignored until recently—by architectural scholars. As with a folk-tale or folk song, the folk traditions of form and construction techniques were handed down generation after generation. Settlers built what they knew—they simply cut down trees and made their cabin of hewn logs in the form they remembered. A cabin is here defined as a structure less than two stories high, while a house is here defined as a structure of two or more stories. The words *house* and *cabin* were used loosely in the eighteenth and nineteenth centuries. A cabin may also be defined as a frontier product—a building that a man could build by himself with a few simple tools. A house, on the other hand, may also be defined as a profes-sional product of a housewright, who has saws, nails, and other tools to produce framing, rafters, trusses, and the like. Dating log buildings ac-cording to changes in size from one to two stories, or by the manner of construction, is unreliable, because the resources of the builder alone account for size and construction.[5] People came to the Valley of Virginia frontier with their architectural ideas already set. Using various forms, they created a building type that was a synthesis of tradition and available materials. To paraphrase Le Corbusier, the log buildings were machines in which to live. Log cabins may be viewed today as historical artifacts, indicators of our American heritage, or as objects of sculpture, but they were basically utilitarian folk forms.

German settlers in eastern Pennsylvania brought with them a tradition of log construction. In William Penn's new colony they encountered the Swedish and Finnish traditions, and all the types of construction merged. Half a century after the Germans arrived, the Scotch-Irish came to Penn-sylvania. In the late nineteenth century the name Scotch-Irish was used to distinguish the earlier settlers from the "famine Irish" immigrants who came later.[6] "Ulster-Scottish" would be a more accurate name than

Scotch-Irish, for these early settlers were descendants of the Scots who had colonized northern Ireland during the religious troubles of Great Britain.

Entering America through the ports of Philadelphia, and New Castle, Delaware, the Scotch-Irish quickly spread west and south. From Lancaster and York counties in Pennsylvania they went south into Maryland, across the Potomac, and into the Valley of Virginia. They took their architectural forms and translated them into log construction. In an illuminating study published in 1939 titled *The Log Cabin Myth*, Harold Shurtleff supplied ample evidence that log construction was first used in the Swedish-German settlements of Delaware in the mid-seventeenth century but did not spread elsewhere until the eighteenth century, when the Scotch-Irish utilized the ideas in settling new frontiers.

The early English settlers of the eastern seaboard colonies rarely constructed log cabins; instead, they constructed temporary shelters and quickly replaced them with framed houses of sawed or hewn timbers. All of the European colonists first built the type of dwelling they were accustomed to at home. The myth persists, however, that the log cabin was the earliest American colonists' home.

In settling the American frontier, the Scotch-Irish used the Scandinavian-German log-construction techniques to build the forms they had always known. Whitewashed inside and out, a Scotch-Irish log cabin showed little apparent difference from dwellings in the settler's homeland other than the material from which it was constructed. The rectangular cabin type prevalent in the southern mountains was basically an Ulster-Connaught rectangle cabin type with an English-Tidewater outside chimney added on.[7] As seen in the Roanoke Valley, the Scotch-Irish cabin form is a single construction unit of less than two stories and built of log. The rectangular shape and the less-than-two-story size is constant—with some variation in overall height, appendages, and notching techniques.

Inside, the typical Scotch-Irish cabin is divided into two rooms by a light partition. The fireplace is in the largest room, and the main door is near the center of the front wall. Opposite front and rear doors are most typical. Usually a boxed-in stair—built in one corner or along one wall—leads to the loft.

Although the log dwelling was not invented by Americans, it still inspires pride in the craftsmanship and inventiveness of our pioneer ancestors. Evolving from Germanic construction and Scotch-Irish shape, the American rectangular log cabin dominated the frontier in the Valley of Virginia.

6

Log Corner-Timbering

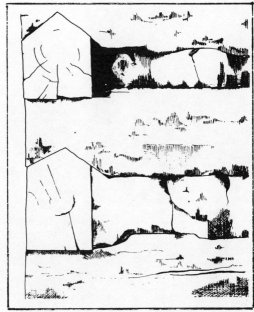

V-notched;

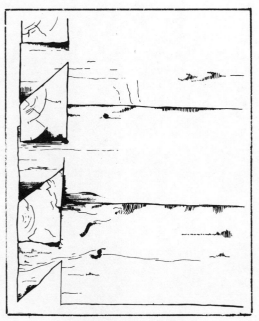

Half-dovetail-notched

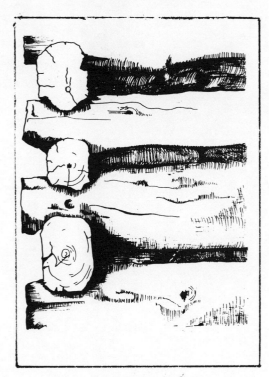

Saddle-notched

7

Rectangular Log Cabin
Route 779, Roanoke County:
Catawba
c. 1825

The typical Valley of Virginia log cabin is one and one-half stories high. Added to over the years with a second chimney, a lean-to, or various sheds, log cabins were sheathed as quickly as possible. Many log cabins are thus difficult to recognize.

8
Square Log Cabin
Intersection of Route 220 and Route 677, Roanoke County
c. 1850

Roughly eighteen feet square, this log cabin near Boones Mill is a unique example of an English shape in the valley. It has a gable roof with an external chimney in the center of one gable end. The front door is located near the center of the front wall, away from the chimney end. Square cabins seldom have front porches, or rear doors, but this one has a rear shed addition with door. Apparently the door was cut later, as it swings out rather than in.

"Square" cabins may actually be slightly rectangular in proportion, but vary by no more than three feet longer than they are wide. Sixteen feet to a side is the normal measurement. These proportions have been traced back to Neolithic, Anglo-Saxon, Medieval, and Tudor England.[1] English influence may also be seen in the external chimney in the center of one gable. The form of the square cabin and the chimney placement came from Tidewater Virginia across the Piedmont to the Blue Ridge, rather than down the Valley of Virginia from Pennsylvania. The square-cabin form is found on the eastern slopes of the Blue Ridge, but it is seldom found in the valley—where the Scotch-Irish who brought Pennsylvania-German influences were dominant. The square form of cabin was called an English cabin by Moravian missionaries as early as 1749. Traveling through Southwest Virginia, the missionaries noted: "In the evening we lodged in an English cabin (thus they call the English houses there)."[2] As with the Pennsylvania form of the rectangular cabin, the square cabin translates the English traditional form of building into the log construction found in America.

9

Log Cabin Plans
Left plan: rectangular, Scotch-Irish cabin; right plan: square, English cabin

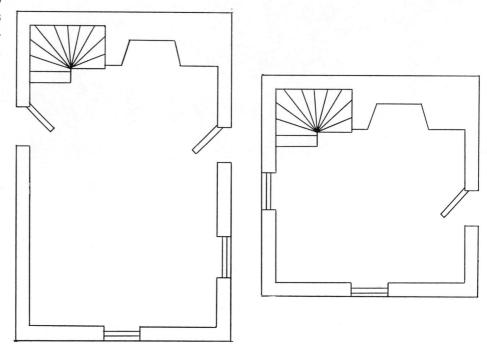

10
Single-Crib Barn
Intersection of Route 614 and Route 677, Roanoke County
c. 1900

Farm culture of the Valley of Virginia prized livestock, so barn architecture was of significant concern. It was necessary that the stock have both shelter and food. The building of barns was based upon two traditions inherent in the Pennsylvania German settler's culture. From the Black Forest of Germany and from Poland came the knowledge of building with horizontal logs notched at the corners. A rectangular construction unit, the single-crib form has been traced to prehistoric Europe through the Bronze Age and the Middle Ages.

Single-crib barns, such as this one in Roanoke County (fig. 10), are used for a wide variety of purposes. Rarely is a single-crib barn the only building on a farm. There were smaller one-level buildings for sheds and storage. Most buildings, however, were of log construction, and some had

21

additions in the form of lean-tos or attached sheds. This Roanoke County barn is a good example of the single-crib log structure without additions, the simplest "Lincoln log" construction with no foundations. The logs are saddle notched (see fig. 6, right) in the crudest manner—creating a structure that grew logically out of a farmer's needs, traditions, and skills. While this building was probably constructed in the late nineteenth or early twentieth century, local tradition relates that some log structures on this property were constructed as late as the 1930s. Construction techniques of log building survived long after houses were constructed in many other ways. Chronologically, local barn building corresponds precisely with economic fluctuations, less precisely with technological changes, and rarely with the overall pattern of architectural style changes.[1] This single-crib barn represents continuation of a long tradition of vernacular building. Often overlooked, the barn—south of Roanoke City in a poor farming area of shale soil and softwood trees—reminds us of older building traditions.

11
Single-Crib Barn
Route 785, Roanoke County
Catawba
c. 1875

In the Pennsylvania tradition, a barn built into the bank allows level access to the upper and lower levels. Sheathing in board and batten indicates a late date for this common outbuilding.

12
Single-Crib Barn
Route 785, Roanoke County
Catawba
c. 1875

Lean-tos, sheds, and other appendages engulf many of the Valley's single-crib barns. A late example here has saddle notches joining the logs of the original structure.

13
Double-Crib Barn
Route 650, Roanoke County: Catawba
c. 1850

The double-crib barn, a form that was known in Northern and Central Europe, was introduced into the valley of Virginia by the Pennsylvania Germans.[1] This form of barn consists of two separate square construction units, called pens or cribs, separated by an open runway or threshing floor. Both units are connected by one common gable roof with a ridgeline running transversely. The barn in figure 13 is a double-crib constructed with a lower level for stock and an upper level for grain and hay storage. Entrance to the lower level was sheltered by a cantilevered forebay, which was often left unsupported. Characteristic of the Roanoke area, the form is built of logs with a variety of notching, but the spaces between the logs are rarely chinked. Vertical boards often covered the log barns.

24

The Catawba barn has a supported forebay on one side, a gable roof, and attached sheds covered by flaring gables. Construction appears crude; the exterior was originally covered with vertical boards in an uneven pattern. The logs are round and joined by saddle notching. Small piles of rocks placed at intervals form the foundation. A distinctive forebay is cantilevered out on the floor joists. Posts, which are later additions, assist in support of the floor. The hinges on the doors have a distinctive Pennsylvania tapered-heart shape.

The bottom level is just six feet high but was, of course, only for the stock. Beneath the main floor there are long floor joists with hand-hewn marks on them. An earthen ramp covered with grass leads to the upper section on the opposite side from the forebay. Through large double doors it is possible to see the massive double-crib log structure with its open center section. Diamond-shaped holes high up in one gable end permit martins and other birds easy entrance and exit.[2]

The logs in the interior of the barn are saddle notched but not chinked. The interior was constructed by an intricate system of balancing one part against the other. Mortise and tenon construction was used only in the frame of the main doorway and in the new addition. Two long ceiling beams—made of more than one log running lengthwise along each side of the cribs—are notched to support the ceiling ribs. There is no ridge pole; the ribs are engaged against each other and pegged. This nineteenth-century structure has one of the best double-crib log interiors in the Roanoke Valley.

14
Double-Crib Barn
Route 785, Roanoke County
Catawba
c. 1875
The log cribs are concealed, as almost all double-crib barns were sheathed over to protect the inner structure from the elements. Many area barns look like this one.

15
Forebay Bank Barn
Midland Road, Salem
c. 1850

Many barns in the Valley of Virginia are derivations of Pennsylvania types. Although the sizes vary greatly, the two-level bank barn (built of stone, brick, frame, or log) with an unsupported forebay is common in the area. If there was no hill for easy access to the second story, an earthen ramp was constructed for access to the threshing floor. Bank barns have cantilevered overhangs on one side; often various appendages were built onto the basic two-level form.

Located almost in the center of Roanoke County, this unusually large wooden barn is one of the area's best examples of barn craftsmanship. The outer shell of the barn is constructed of sheathed beams. Surprisingly, the inside has the familiar double-crib log structure joined by V-notching, hewn and constructed in the same manner as the double-crib barns in Catawba. The barn's exterior takes the form of a Pennsylvania bank barn. With its traditional double-crib form, the interior integrates the building with the Roanoke County region. In Roanoke County traditional patterns in vernacular architecture often persist.

26

16
Bake Oven
Old Route 311, Roanoke County: Hanging Rock
c. 1850

Located in the Hanging Rock area of Roanoke County, this bake oven represents a Pennsylvania-German form seldom found so far south. Unfortunately, the building (perhaps an inn) that the oven served has disappeared. Also found in Central Europe, Scandinavia, and Switzerland, this type of bake oven is a continuation of prehistoric folk forms. The oven measures five feet high by six and a half feet wide at the base, with an opening for the door fifteen inches by nineteen inches. The depth is eighty-eight inches. This structure was a simple but efficient outdoor oven.

No German farmstead in the eighteenth and nineteenth century was complete without a bake oven, for every family then did its own baking.

27

In the Pennsylvania German region, outdoor ovens were one of the first requisites for a new home. Most ovens were made of a combination of stone and brick, as here, with the iron door at one end and the chimney at the other. The ovens were lined with brick normally; later examples were lined with iron. The sides, back, and front were usually enclosed within a frame structure. Often three or four feet of roof extended at the front end to provide a shelter area. On the side of this enclosure were shelves. An open space between the oven and the roof provided ventilation. The original frame structure at Hanging Rock has disappeared, so what is seen today is simply a covering to protect the oven from the elements.

An outdoor oven was safer than an indoor fireplace bake oven, and it also eliminated intense heat in a kitchen during the summer. A fire was built directly on the floor. The temperature could be regulated by adjustments to the door or the damper. Ovens were used to bake supplies of bread, pies, cakes, and meat, as well as to dry fruits and vegetables for the winter. A long iron scraper was used to pull out ashes, and the bread was moved in and out of the oven by means of a shovellike tool with a wooden handle, called a peel. Inside cook stoves and kitchen ranges gradually supplanted outdoor bake ovens. Today most outdoor ovens have been neglected or torn down. The bake oven at Hanging Rock is a unique southern survival of a significant American folk form.[1]

17
Overhang Outbuilding
Brick Springhouse at Pleasant Grove
Route 11, Roanoke County: Glenvar
After 1853

An unusual brick springhouse, with water still flowing through it, this
structure is one of the outbuildings still functioning at Pleasant Grove (see
fig. 81). It is a particularly interesting outbuilding because it helps to define the folk approach to architecture. Many outbuildings in this form may
be seen all over rural areas of southwest Virginia, with many survivals in
the Roanoke Valley. The folk builder constructed in the old manner because that was what he knew, and he felt that traditional patterns were
the best. Form rarely changes in a folk building, despite shifts in material
and decoration.

The springhouse is a classic example of a distinctive folk-building form.
The most outstanding characteristic is the gable roof carried forward over

29

the door for five feet. Similar overhang structures were known in early Neolithic Europe and were common through the Iron Age. The structures were built of log, clay, stone, or vertical posts in the ground. While the connection between prehistoric and modern types is tenuous, the form still exists in central Europe and Scandinavia today. Built there of horizontal log or stone, these buildings serve as houses, barns, bake ovens, buildings for drying crops, smokehouses, and, in Finland, as saunas.[1] Emigrants from Europe brought folk forms to the colonies. In the Roanoke Valley overhang outbuildings were constructed of log, frame, stone, brick, or even modern cinder blocks and were used for a variety of farm outbuildings. The fact that a building in this form has been constructed in this century does not lessen its importance as a folk object. Folk architecture carries on traditional forms.

18
Overhang Outbuilding
Route 620, Roanoke County
Catawba
c. 1850
Unique among log buildings, this cantilevered springhouse has survived and is still used for storage. Essentially, this building consists of one log box on top of a smaller log box that encloses a spring.

19
Overhang Outbuilding (detail)
Route 620, Roanoke County
Catawba
c. 1850

Two forms of notching may be seen here. On the lower structure the unusual half-dovetail form of notching indicates a high degree of craftsmanship, seldom seen on log structures in the Valley. Supported on two cantilevered logs, the upper portion of this structure exhibits the normal V-notching, which is prevalent on Roanoke Valley log structures. Both types of notching were self-draining and durable.

20
Overhang Outbuilding
Route 612, Roanoke County
Wabun
c. 1850

A smokehouse of V-notched logs uses the ancient overhang form for practicality. This surviving building is noteworthy because of the structure built on top of the log smokehouse to protect the farm bell.

Overhang Outbuilding
1402 Grandin Road Extension
S.W., Roanoke City
c. 1850

Constructed of brick laid in American bond and with an interesting molded cornice above, this little outbuilding may have served a variety of purposes.

Overhang Outbuilding
Route 779, Roanoke County
Catawba
c. 1900

Made of commercially milled lumber, outbuildings in the traditional form continued to be constructed well into the twentieth century. A farmer added little buildings such as this one to his homestead as needed.

Overhang Outbuilding
Route 620, Roanoke County
Catawba
c. 1950

Folk forms are often continued with the use of new technologies and new materials. Mass-produced cinder blocks were used here in the creation of an outbuilding form that is centuries old.

24
Tobacco Barn
Route 701, Roanoke County: Catawba
c. 1875

This building, made of logs connected by V-notching, remains one of the
few tobacco barns in the valley. Measuring fourteen feet high to the roof
rafters and twenty feet long on each side, the structure has a completely
open interior. The single low entrance led to the fire area. Holes for rods,
from which the curing tobacco hung, dot numerous levels.

In Roanoke County the growing and processing of tobacco in the late
nineteenth century prevailed more than most people realize. Tobacco
served as the main cash crop for many of the small farmers. The tobacco
barn epitomizes a distinctive form associated with an important agricultural and economic era. In contrast to the great numbers of tobacco barns

still standing in nearby Franklin County or, of course, in North Carolina, there are few tobacco barns left in the Roanoke area.

Logs about seven inches in diameter divided the interior of local tobacco barns into four levels about four feet wide, with tie poles about one-half the size of the logs. Layers of poles further divided the space to the roof. A roof covered with boards, except for an opening for smoke, finished off the top. Chinking—along with a closely fitted little door—made the building as airtight as possible.[1]

Despite some variations in the overall form, the layers of poles on which the tobacco hung for fire curing are found inside most tobacco barns. Most tobacco in Roanoke County was fire cured. Hung over a fire of hardwood and sawdust, it absorbed aromas from the smoke. Before it is cured, green tobacco consists of 80 to 90 percent water. Curing removes the water and causes chemical changes that give the leaves a certain character.[2] Curing can make a good crop or can ruin it; the farmer cannot market his crop until it has been properly cured. He must have a well-functioning barn, because the best grade of tobacco depends heavily on proper curing. The crop is then sold at auction warehouses.

The tobacco crop returned a high income per acre. Despite the fact that tobacco growing debilitated the soil, many farmers in the nineteenth and early twentieth centuries depended heavily on tobacco for their main source of cash. In 1840, for instance, Roanoke County production included 599,000 pounds of tobacco.[3] The surviving tobacco barn in Catawba is a good example of a functional building of a distinctive type that was once found throughout the Valley.

25
Stone House (with brick addition)
Old Hershberger Road, Roanoke County
c. 1797 (c. 1825)

The stone part of this building may be one of the earliest homes left in the Roanoke Valley. This section is a two-story structure following the English tradition of house building. It has been called a one-over-one because one room is on top of another. Quite often these buildings were expanded, as here, by the addition of another section to increase the living space. The use of limestone in the early section is particularly unusual for the Roanoke Valley. The brick section, an early example of the I-form, has Flemish bond on all sides, with bricks of an unusually large size and a particularly fine molded brick cornice. The stone chimney of the original portion was opened to serve the new addition on the other side. The front porch dates from the twentieth century.

Samuel Harshberger, son of a German immigrant who had lived in Pennsylvania, may have built the stone section. His name is perpetuated in a number of places in the northwestern part of the city and county, but the spelling was changed to Hershberger. (Early clerks in Augusta and Botetourt counties, where the oldest Roanoke County records are located, often used phonetic spellings of German names in recording and indexing.) Samuel Harshberger purchased 504 acres from a Francis Graham in 1793.[1] After Harshberger purchased the property, the first significant change in his tax occurs in 1798.[2] According to the writers of the WPA History of Roanoke,[3] the house was built in 1797; this date is said to have been seen on the north stone gable. Unfortunately, a large vine growing into the mortar surrounding the stones today obscures the north gable. The 1798 tax change perhaps best indicates that construction of the stone portion of the house was finished by then. In the early nineteenth century the brick addition was built.

35

26
I-Form House (Speedwell)
6135 Merriman Road, Roanoke County: Starkey
c. 1831

Speedwell exemplified a classic Virginia I house. The letter I describes the shape and the plan of the main body of this type of house. A rectangular block with a pitched roof and gables on the ends, the building form is one room deep and two rooms long. Generally the I-house has a center entrance and often a center stair-hall. A back door is usually opposite the front door on the long back of the building. In most examples evenly spaced windows flank a central front door. Providing good ventilation, the I-form house was prevalent from the late eighteenth century to the early twentieth century in southeastern America. The form is common in Tidewater Virginia, the Piedmont of Virginia and North Carolina, the bluegrass areas of Kentucky and Tennessee, and in the lower Midwest. Often overlooked by architectural historians, the I-house is the most distinctive and recognizable architectural form in the Valley of Virginia. The Roanoke area contains many examples, not only in rural areas but also in the suburbs and occasionally even within urban developments.

While the I is extremely common in nineteenth century America, its origins are obscured in English and European folk building. The Georgian two-story, four-room plan (two rooms deep with a central hall) influenced the development of the I-form in the early eighteenth century. I-houses seem to use the front half of this Georgian plan.

A Roanoke County description of an I-form house was found in the 1843 will of Henry Snider, in which he divides his house between two of his heirs.

> I give to my dearly beloved wife Catharine Snider the East end of the house I now live in embracing one room and a passage on the lower floor and two rooms and a passage on the upper floor with so much of the lot equal to the width of the house, back, to the land of Nathaniel Burwick. . . .
>
> To my son Henry Snider Jr. the balance of the house I now live in not before giving to my wife as above mentioned being the West end with one room on the lower floor and two rooms on the upper floor with the right and free use of the passages, stairs and outdoors to pass through.[1]

Although often made of brick in the Roanoke Valley (as at Speedwell), I-houses more commonly used wood weatherboards over frame and sometimes even over logs. Even under modern layers of asbestos or aluminum siding, soft-drink signs, bricktex, or the like, the I-shape is always obvious, whatever the size. A basic I with a kitchen wing forming an L-shape or a T-shape is common to the region, too. Often an I house has many appendages, such as porches, sheds, and garages, but the basic form remains recognizable. I houses commonly have sheds or ells on the rear. The I-house ell normally faces east or south to get the sun, and its front looks toward the road to present the best image to the public.

The building material—whether log, brick, or stone—exerted no influence on the I-form. The builder determined all the internal and external shapes prior to building. His mental geometry came first,[2] then ornament—which was optional and not part of the primary planning. Secondary embellishments do not change the basic idea. As styles such as Greek Revival and Gothic came and went in the nineteenth century, the basic form remained. Decoration on I-houses, however, is extremely unreliable for dating purposes. For instance, at Speedwell, built in 1831, Gustavus Sedon constructed a Greek Revival porch and doorcase (fig. 27) on the I form in 1877.[3] Local builders, of course, influenced the final product, but they stayed within the general form, which accounts for similarities within an area in spite of decorational differences.

After the Civil War a gable was often integrated into the center of the facade of new I-houses. Sometimes a gable was even added to an older I to bring it up-to-date. The resulting house—called by the ungainly title triple-A I house because of its three gables, or A's—differs from the earlier I's that had only two gables, or A's, at each end. The later I's with three gables have an overhanging roof at the gable ends and often a variety of decoration on differently proportioned center gables. At the time of these innovations, chimneys became smaller and were built inside to accommodate stoves. The center gable of the triple-A I was probably derived from Gothic Revival handbooks and a desire to elaborate the folk form with up-to-date decoration. This elaborated form of the I house is one of the South's most visible house types.

Columns and other frills to create a "plantation house" often decorated the I. Used by prosperous English and Scotch-Irish landowners for many generations, the dressed-up I is common to the valley today. The I-house often shows the prosperity of a rural area and financial success in an agrarian society.[4] The new social ordering of the nineteenth century was represented by the commanding presence of the I house with its long rooms arranged to create the largest possible facade facing the road; indeed, this house was the symbol of economic stability and prosperity—bourgeois respectability—in rural, agricultural societies.

Speedwell was built by Lewis Harvey (1785–1842). In 1819 he acquired a 7,000 acre tract in the south part of Roanoke County. Harvey built a furnace for iron production near what is now the village of Starkey. As a result of the abundant supply of brown hematite found in the area, the Harvey Furnace soon gained a reputation for producing iron of very high quality. Based on tax and land records that show an increase of $1500 in Harvey's tax valuation,[5] his house was completed by 1831. Soon afterwards, the house was named for the English ship, the *Speedwell*, that according to family tradition brought Harvey's ancestors to America. Lewis Harvey died without leaving a will, so an inventory was made of his personal possessions.

Inventories illuminate architectural studies. Inventorying is an ancient idea made legal by Henry VIII, who decreed that the probating of wills in ecclesiastical courts could only be authorized after an inventory of a deceased's possessions was made. Such an inventory had to be taken by two disinterested, reputable people. Prevention of tax evasion was probably the major purpose of the statute. In Roanoke County in the nineteenth century, when a person died without a will, the laws of Virginia required that an appraisal be made within four months. The court appointed the appraisers, paid them one dollar a day, and accepted their evidence. Two or three appraisers went to a house soon after a person's death and recorded the contents of each room. Sometimes they listed objects by each room, other times they merely grouped objects. The appraisers also went to sheds, barns, and outbuildings to note their contents and to estimate the cash value of each item. Valuations often appear haphazard—indicating more about the appraisers than about the actual worth of objects. The appraisers undervalued many things, probably to lower taxes; or perhaps the appraisers had little idea of the real worth of household possessions. On the other hand, valuations of crops, land, and animals were usually more accurate. Despite the fact that the appraisers' attitude toward the person whose estate they were inventorying may have colored their judgment, the importance of an inventory must not be overlooked. The listing of beds, for instance, may reveal that there were not enough beds for each person known to be living in a house; several people sleeping on one bed must have been common.

After Lewis Harvey's death, his personal property was appraised and recorded March 21, 1842.[6] The extremely complete listing gives a good picture of the contents of a Virginia I home during the mid-1800s. Typical home furnishings of a well-to-do merchant in Roanoke County are detailed in the first 63 items. After these, the list continues with things such as barrels, buckets, fat cans, and old iron, which were probably the contents of storerooms or sheds.

Henrietta Powers Harvey, granddaughter of Lewis Harvey, married Taswell Merriman Starkey, and they lived at Speedwell. In 1877, Starkey contracted for remodeling work on Speedwell with Gustavus Sedon, a Roanoke carpenter. Sedon's account book detailing his transactions between the years 1852 and 1886 offers insights into local building. Sedon (1820–93), a German immigrant, is first noted in the Roanoke area in the 1850 census. He worked on many of the outstanding buildings in the valley. As a handyman-carpenter, Sedon installed windows, built simple structures, and added wooden details to buildings under construction.

In May 1877 an entry in Sedon's journal appears under the name "T. M. Starke." It reads, "for contract work to your hous [*sic*] $680 . . . to put on your hous 20 qu [quires] slate—$20." The unusual doorcase at Speedwell looks heavy-handed and Germanic—the style of Sedon's work. Some of the door details at Speedwell resemble those at Pleasant Grove, for which records firmly show that Sedon did the work. The marked similarity between the back-porch columns on Hollins College's Main Dormitory (for which records also show that Sedon was the carpenter) and the front-porch columns at Speedwell, confirms that Sedon built Speedwell's columns. Some of Sedon's work on Speedwell consisted of the construction of the portico. The slate roof noted in Sedon's journal is still in place.[7]

1842 inventory and appraisal of the household property belonging to the estate of Lewis Harvey

1 pair andirons	$ .75
1 pair shovel and tongs	1.50
1 walnut bureau	9.00
1 walnut press	5.00
1 walnut candlestand	2.00
1 brass 8 day clock	40.00
1 small walnut table	1.50
1 oval looking glass	5.00
20 split-bottom chairs	5.00
2 pair brass candlesticks	2.50
3 pair candle snuffers	.75
1 lot of books	20.00
1 walnut [*illegible*]	2.00
3 window curtains	.75
1 wagon whip	.75
1 lot of tinware	.75
4 pair andirons	1.50
2 Liverpool pitchers	1.25
6 silver table spoons	15.00
10 silver tea spoons	7.00
2 wash bowls	1.00
3 doz. willow plates	4.00
4 doz. [*illegible*]	1.00
22 glass tumblers	2.75
10 stone jars	5.00
6 D Milk pans	1.50
5 crocks	.42
2 stake dishes	4.00
4 dishes	3.00
1 dish	.25
1 bell metal kettle	2.00
1 copper kettle	2.00
1 tea board and china ware	3.00
1 bell knife box, tin pan etc.	1.50
2 tea kettle trivets and pot	2.00
2 sets knives and forks	1.00
1 tin baker	1.50

1 side table and w. bucket	1.25
1 secretary and book case	18.00
1 walnut press	12.00
1 walnut dining table and cover	6.00
7 pair pillow cases	3.50
16 towels	3.50
9 table cloths	18.00
3 preserve dishes	2.00
1 hatchet	.37½
1 bed, bedstead and furniture	20.00
1 trunnel [*sic*] bed, bedstead and furniture	5.00
1 small pine table	.13
1 bedstead, bed and furniture	20.00
1 bedstead, bed and furniture	15.00
1 toilet table and cover	2.50
1 dressing glass	2.00
4 window curtains	.80
1 trunnel [*sic*] bed and furniture	12.00
7 pair cotton sheets and linen	14.00
2 small counterpanes—fringed	5.00
5 large counterpanes—fringed	25.00
1 counterpane and pillows	4.00
1 crib and tick	.63
1 flax wheel	1.50
1 wash stand	.50
1 clothes press	1.25

27
Speedwell (porch detail)
6135 Merriman Road
Roanoke County: Starkey
Porch 1877
This Greek Revival–style porch and doorcase were built by Gustavus Sedon (1820–93) in 1877 for T. M. Starkey, as noted in Sedon's journal.

28

Speedwell (detail)
6135 Merriman Road
Roanoke County: Starkey
c. 1831

This view, looking from one parlor through the center stair-hall into the other parlor, shows the typical I-house plan. Doors, chair rail, paneling, banister, and newel post are all original.

29

Speedwell (detail)
6135 Merriman Road
Roanoke County: Starkey
c. 1831

Even though Speedwell was a substantial home for 1831, its interior woodwork was remarkably simple. Light and delicate, the fireplace here reflects earlier design ideas.

30

I-Form House (Belmont)
Ole Monterey Golf Course
N.E., Roanoke City
c. 1800

On property originally owned by Col. William Fleming (1728–95), a local Revolutionary War figure, this one-and-a-half-story log structure has two almost-square rooms on either side of a central hall. Made of squared logs, V-notched, with wide spaces between, it has a double-stepped chimney on either end. It is shown in this picture (taken c. 1930) without later sheathing and enclosed porch.

I-Form House
Left plan: I-form house
Right plan: ⅔ I-form house

The house commonly found in this area is the I-form house with a central hall and equal-size rooms on either side. Upstairs, the plan is the same. Sometimes the I was built without one-third of the plan, creating a two-thirds I as seen in figure 32.

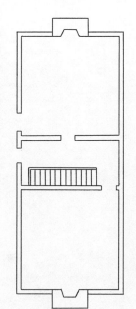
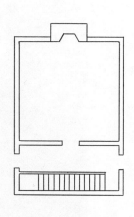

32

I-Form House
429 Cleveland Avenue, Salem
c. 1850

Only two-thirds of the I plan has been used here in a variation of the form. The center hall, with stairway and a room on one side, was all that the builder could afford. The portion he did build conforms to the folk tradition, however, and is as well built as a normal full-I-form house.

33

I-Form House
110 High Street, Salem
c. 1855

A long rectangular mass, low hip roof, chimneys at both ends, and a portico that is one-third the length of the house make up the typical Valley of Virginia I-form house. With its two-story porch and wooden millwork decoration, the house appears to be more than a simple folk manifestation decorated in the Greek Revival manner.

I-Form House
335 High Street, Salem
c. 1860

The variety of decorations on I houses in Salem is remarkable. Here, the standard I has received a bracketed cornice and unusual carvings around the porch and over the windows.

I-Form House (detail)
335 High Street, Salem
c. 1860

A novel lintel on this I-form house is typical of the inventiveness of local interpreters of handbook designs. The anonymous carver has given this lintel an Egyptian feeling with its sunburst and curved-form cross. Unfortunately, there is no documentation about the craftsman.

36
I-Form House
Intersection of Route 221 and
Route 690, Roanoke County
Poage's Mill
c. 1860

Prosperous farmers would add as much decoration to their I-form house as they could afford. The two-story columns, and the flush boards in the center of this unusually long I house, indicate the owner's prosperity.

37
I-Form House
Intersection of Route 221 and
Route 694, Roanoke County
c. 1860

The double porch under the eave of this I-form house indicates that the porch was designed with the house. The porch form is typical of houses found in very warm climates.

38
I-Form House
979 Lauderdale Avenue
Vinton
c. 1860

Often the I-form house was constructed in a very simple manner. Here, despite a twentieth-century doorway, is the most common, basic, one-room-deep dwelling of this area.

**I-Form House
Hollins College Campus
Route 11, Roanoke County
c. 1870**

The interior chimneys and front gable mark the late-nineteenth-century I-form house. Molded clapboard and horizontal proportions also indicate the late nineteenth century. Millwork decoration was probably produced locally.

**I-Form House
825 Virginia Avenue, Salem
c. 1870**

In the latter part of the nineteenth century a center gable was often added to the I-form house, making the structure into what historians of folk architecture have called a triple-A I. The A-shape of the gables gives the name. This type of house generally has late-nineteenth-century-style decorations and internal chimneys.

**I-Form House
202 North Broad Street, Salem
c. 1870**

The late-nineteenth-century I-form house has millwork decoration under its gables. Often the same millwork may be seen on a variety of houses. The porch here is a later addition.

42

I-Form House (detail)
220 North Broad Street, Salem
c. 1870

A triple-A I house here shows a variety of decorations with millwork cutouts in the gable (exactly the same form as 202 North Broad Street, Salem; see fig. 41). Italianate hooded windows, fine cast-iron railing, and Ionic columns supporting the porch are all typical of late-nineteenth-century style eclectism and its factory-made architectural embellishments.

43

I-Form House
228 Richfield Avenue, Salem
c. 1870

High on a hill overlooking the town of Salem, this I-form house has been ornamented with Italianate brackets, window lintels, and cut-out designs around the porch. Despite the projection for front-door hall and upstairs hall, the standard Valley of Virginia I-form has been retained.

44
**I-Form House
6933 Thirlane Road, Roanoke
County: Kingston
c. 1875**

Despite asbestos siding and a 1920s front porch, the distinctive I-shape may be seen here with a hip roof and gable on top. Interior chimneys indicate a late date for this house.

45
**I-Form House
5621 Plantation Road, Roanoke
County
c. 1875**

The I-form with a perpendicular rear extension, giving the building an L shape, is often seen in this area. Ornamental window lintels here have beaded decoration similar to that attributed to Gustavus Sedon. The front porch has been considerably changed since the house was built.

46
**I-Form House, outbuildings
5621 Plantation Road, Roanoke
County
c. 1875**

The original outbuildings may still be found clustered around the well at the rear of this house. Kitchen, smokehouse, quarters, and other service buildings have survived into the twentieth century.

47
I-Form Houses
206 and 202 Academy Street
Salem
c. 1880

This matched pair of I houses was probably built by Charles M. Dulaney, a plasterer and/or Noah Hockman, a carpenter and builder. The two houses were constructed during Salem's boom period after the Civil War.

48
I-Form House
Route 711, east of junction with Route 612, Roanoke County: Bent Mountain
c. 1880

The traditional I-form house, here with the triple-A gables, was covered with a variety of late-nineteenth-century decorative forms. Sheathed in three varieties of clapboarding, this house shows the Queen-Anne-style interest in texture. The wraparound porch with cutoff corners and ornate cutout work, the brackets at the eaves and the points of the gable, are all manifestations of the Queen Anne style also.

49
I-Form House
316 Broad Street, Salem
c. 1885

If the Eastlake-style turnings on the porch, the two leaded-glass bay windows with brackets above, and the little octagonal tower were pared away, a standard Valley of Virginia I-form house would remain.

50
Hall-and-Parlor House
Route 785, near junction with Route 650, Roanoke County: Catawba
1850

Another example of a folk form, this log hall-and-parlor-plan house features two downstairs rooms, each with its own entrance and separated with a log partition. The house has two stories, with a gable roof and two stone chimneys. The north chimney is built of flat shale quarried out of a nearby creek, and the south chimney is built of fieldstone from the land. Both chimneys are particularly well constructed for the area. A small window in the south gable lets in light for the attic, and another window below, on the first story, allows light next to the fireplace in the original parlor. Interestingly enough, the wide boards that form the ceiling of the front porch are painted a light blue, to resemble the color of the sky. Persistent folklore holds that mosquitoes will never bite under an open sky; consequently, porch ceilings are painted a distinctive light blue: "The most popular paint color for porch ceilings was a sky blue, a tradition common to many sub-tropical and tropical regions of the world."[1] This traditional paint color was also encountered on the ceiling of a kitchen at 7 Charlotte Square, Edinburgh, Scotland, designed by Robert Adam in 1791, and porch ceilings painted this color may still be seen throughout the southeastern United States.

Inside, despite later changes, some beaded woodwork of yellow poplar remains. The smoothing marks of a hand plane still show on the poplar boards, as well as some traces of old whitewash. In the attic the oak rafters display the marks of a vertical saw. The owner of the house in 1979 remembered an early waterpowered sawmill a few miles down the road in what is now Montgomery County.[2] Rafters (fig. 51) meet in open mortise joints held together with wooden pins—there is no ridge pole—collar beams support each set of rafters.[3] The handcraftsmanship still evident in this house makes it one of the area's most important survivals.

Originally detached a log kitchen stood behind the house, but an attached kitchen wing has replaced it. Several outbuildings randomly sit on the hill behind the house, and there is a modern cinder-block springhouse at the nearby spring. In 1979 the owner clearly remembered a log springhouse, "which was built and rebuilt after each flood."[4]

The main house and its surrounding outbuildings are ideally sited, as were so many nineteenth-century houses (fig. 52). The home, set into a hillside, has a windbreak of trees behind, a spring beside, a view of crops and pasture in front, and a stream and road beyond. Houses such as this were often placed very carefully at the junction of a floodplain and a hillside. In folk tradition, utility was more important for a site than beauty. Natural features are used, not for their visual appeal, but rather for conservation of energy and the creation of harmony in the natural environment.[5]

Many factors determine the site of a folk house: water (subsurface and surface), slope, location of workable land, soil and vegetation, rock outcroppings, erosion, aspect, or exposure, prevailing winds, visual qualities, and accessibility to roads.[6] The skill in choosing a site dates back at least to Roman settlements in England (c. 40 A.D.–400 A.D.). The Romans tended, writes a noted historian, "to select a rather special type of site: a valley slope facing south or east, not too high up, with shelter from the wind, exposure to the sun, and water close at hand."[7] Such a description fits the Catawba Valley hall-and-parlor house perfectly.

A spring with good gravity flow lies within a few yards of the back door of this hall-and-parlor house. The aspect of the building is protected from west and northwest winds by the hill above, but the site is accessible from nearby roads. Within the rock outcroppings of the hills, a place requiring minimum excavation was found. Finally, the house is situated above the creek with fields and pasture in view from the porch.[8]

According to the 1979 owner, his ancestors came from Pennsylvania and started building on the site. In the mid-nineteenth century many Pennsylvanians settled in the Catawba Valley. The first reference found for this land appears in the tax record for 1835 in the Montgomery County Courthouse in Christiansburg.[9] The southwestern section of Catawba, where this house is located along the North Fork of the Roanoke River, was part of Montgomery County until it was annexed by Roanoke County in 1849. The 1837 tax records of Montgomery County list the land as owned by George Surface, who lived in Indiana. In February of 1838 he sold the property, with a building (probably a log structure) valued at $80, to John Hambrick.[10] The 1837 building may be part of the present structure. During Hambrick's ownership the tax valuation for buildings went up to $200, doubtlessly for improvements to the log building or for other buildings on the property. In 1848 Peter Surface, the next owner, sold to John F. Bennett et al.[11] In 1849 Griffith John purchased eighty acres, "more or less" of this land from John Bennett et al., "with its appertenances."[12]

According to 1849 tax records in Roanoke County, Griffith John's tax bill included $150 worth of buildings on the property. Roanoke County annexed a part of Montgomery County in 1849, so John's lower evaluation of buildings represents Roanoke County's assessment. In 1850 Griffith John had $250 more added to his tax evaluation, so that was probably the year when the present house was built, or was substantially remodeled into its present form.[13] Between 1851 and 1856 John's tax value remained the same. In 1857, $100 more was added, again for buildings; this value of $500 continued through the 1860s. The 1979 owner of the house was a direct descendant of Griffith John.

Griffith John died October 29, 1883, at the age of seventy-eight. He lies buried in the family cemetery on the hill near his house, and his stone records his dates. The inventory[14] recorded on November 29, 1883, because he left no will, offers a clear picture of furnishings at that date. Presumably most of the furniture had been in John's possession for many years. The contents listed portray the spartan, simple way of life in this rural area. Farm implements, grouped by barns and outbuildings, were listed first, then the house contents were noted item by item.

The first item—a cooking stove valued at $10, one of the more expensive items on the inventory—was probably made of iron. Much a part of Germanic tradition, it shows technological advancement beyond an open fireplace.[15] Next listed was "1 Lot Table Ware and table" worth $3. A kitchen cupboard valued at $2 probably served as a storage area. One lot of crocks at $1.50 and six "old chairs" at $.25 each were used in the kitchen. One table valued at $.50 must have been very crude. A falling-leaf table at $4, a corner cupboard at $5, and a candlestand at $1 were probably better quality pieces of furniture for the parlor. A $2 chest was perhaps a simple blanket chest form. A half dozen "Old Chairs" were noted as kitchen furniture, but six other old chairs, valued again at $.25 each, must have been scattered around the house. Twelve other chairs were valued at $1 apiece and must have been of considerably higher quality. In today's era of careful furniture arrangement, it is hard to comprehend that this little house contained two dozen chairs. Griffith John owned one clock valued at $3—it may have been in the room with his $15 sideboard. The sideboard, perhaps in an ornate Victorian style, was surely a prized possession.

Beds and bed furnishings represented more than half the total value of the contents of the house. One bed and bedding (most likely the master bed), with its accoutrements was valued at $20, the item with the second highest price in the whole inventory. (The highest priced item was a wagon with running gear valued at $60. Many tools listed on the inventory would indicate that Griffith John was a wagonmaker.) The next bedding item was inventoried at $15, "Less the stead"—meaning it was without structure. The next bed had its stead but was also listed at $15. There were eight coverlets, six bed blankets, and one quilt. Surprisingly, the quilt was valued lowest, at $1, the blankets at $1.50, and the coverlets at $3 each. The inventory of Griffith John's possessions in his house ends with one large bell valued at $3 and a $5 shotgun.

The hall-and-parlor house form, similar to the one Griffith John left to his descendants, has a long history in Roanoke County and can be traced, as can the I house and the rectangular log cabin, down the Valley of Virginia into North Carolina. The basic characteristic of this type of house is that a front door opens into the kitchen, which has a fireplace (fig. 53). The kitchen runs the depth of the house, and beside it is another room, also the depth of the house, that may be divided into two rooms. The form may be built of log, brick, or stone; as in other folk forms, the material does not matter. Also, the building may be one, one and one-half, or two stories high. As styles changed, the hall-and-parlor exterior was modified, but the interior divisions remained the same. The facade became symmetrical, with a center door, or often two doors, but the old plan remains inside.

Hall-and-Parlor House (detail)
Route 785, near junction with
Route 650, Roanoke County
Catawba
1850

Where the collar beam meets the rafter with a lap joint, a square wooden pin has been driven into a round hole, locking the collar beam to the rafter. Note the hand-cut wood. The sheathing, now underneath a tin roof, is original.

Hall-and-Parlor House
Route 785, near junction with
Route 650, Roanoke County
Catawba
1850

Located with great care at the junction of the floodplain of the North Fork and a hillside, this hall-and-parlor house sits within a windbreak of trees. Next to a spring with a view of crops and pasture, the house was carefully related to the landscape.

Hall-and-Parlor House (plan)
Derived from Pennsylvania-German forms, the hall-and-parlor house may be recognized by its distinctive entrance into the "hall," or kitchen. The parlor is beside the kitchen.

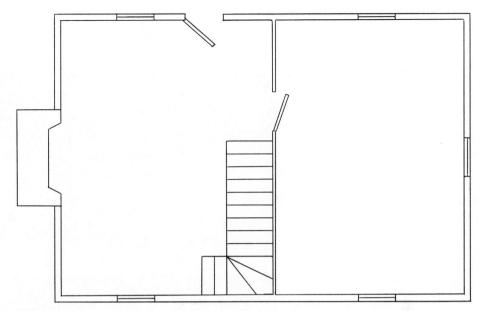

Hall-and-Parlor House
42 East Main Street, Salem
c. 1820

One of the older buildings in Salem, this house may be dated with some precision by the early cut nails found in the attic. The extended gable terminating in an ear form is unusual for this area. Inside, the original hall-and-parlor plan has been greatly altered. The porch is a twentieth-century addition.

55

Hall-and-Parlor House
Route 785, Roanoke County
Catawba
c. 1825

The hall-and-parlor form here was identified by a light partition inside, which was made of hand-planed boards. Now missing its sheathing, some of the original diagonally laid wood chinking is still visible between V-notched logs.

56

Hall-and-Parlor House (detail)
Route 785, Roanoke County
Catawba
c. 1825

Between the logs of dwellings, chinking was necessary to retain warmth. Pieces of wood left over from squaring the trees were wedged diagonally between the logs. Small holes were filled with stones or other material and sealed with mud daubing before sheathing was added.

57

Hall-and-Parlor House
Route 779, Roanoke County
Catawba
c. 1875

Traditional-form houses were often updated with modern front porches; jigsaw cutout work was added here after the Civil War. The earlier stone chimney survives—as does a log cabin behind, which is now joined to create a double house.

58
Spring Resort Buildings
Roanoke Red Sulphur Springs
Route 320, Roanoke County: Catawba (on the grounds of Catawba Hospital)
c. 1856

Two structures survive from this original resort complex: a two-story hotel building and an octagonal gazebo. The once thriving spa sported rambling residence buildings for the infirm, honeymooners, and socialites, who flocked there in the late nineteenth century. The remaining cottage with galleries on the front and back is typical of spring architecture throughout southwestern Virginia and West Virginia.

As early as the eighteenth century, rows of simple log cabins clustered around Virginia mineral springs. Later, during the nineteenth century, large main hotel buildings, sometimes two stories in height, dominated the grounds. The first floor housed a dining room and a ballroom; above were bedrooms. A group of guest cottages, usually two stories high with upper and lower galleries, surrounded the main building in a semicircle, or U-form. These ancillary buildings were remarkably similar throughout the springs resorts, as the buildings at Roanoke Red Sulphur Springs and at Hollins College East Dormitory show. The rows of cottages, with their double galleries, contained simple rooms, each heated by a fireplace. Usually there were two rooms on each side of a center hallway, which connected the front and back galleries for traffic flow and ventilation.

Despite much laudatory literature about hospitality at various springs, some nineteenth-century writing leaves a different impression. Visiting Virginia springs in 1870, Edward A. Pollard noted that the traveler's

> . . . difficulty will be as to the comforts and accommodations of these places. The hotel accommodations of the springs of Virginia are generally insufficient or imperfect or unattractive. [These] places, however blessed and adorned by nature, . . . [have] only a dreary hotel of whitewashed boards, and some thin cottages uniformed with wooden washstands, bare floors and cheap, crying bedsteads.[1]

Roanoke Red Sulphur Springs, on the other hand, was described in glowing terms in a pamphlet prepared to accompany an album of lithographed views of Virginia by Edward Beyer.

> This delightful watering place is situated in the beautiful Catawba Valley, in the county of Roanoke.
>
> Known and visited for many years by a few who were invited to it by the medicinal virtues of its waters, it attracted the attention of an enterprising company, who within the last two years have [sic] erected these magnificent buildings of modern style of architecture, and tastefully improved its natural advantages. Under their control it has become one of the most pleasant summer retreats in the mountains of Virginia.
>
> The improvements consist of a well arranged Hotel, 75 feet in length, handsome cottages, and neat, rural cabins, all combining comfort with beauty of construction.
>
> The water of purest sulphur, rises up in a bold stream, and flows into a marble basin eight or ten feet from the bed of the spring.
>
> In a grove of large forest trees, and fanned by the

> mountain breeze, it is pleasantly cool at all hours in
> the hottest days of the season.
>
> The Roanoke Red is ten miles from the Salem De-
> pot on the Virginia and Tennessee Rail Road, and di-
> rectly on the nearest and best route for southern
> travelers to the Greenbrier White Sulphur. An ample
> supply of coaches, and teams are always in readiness.
> The road abounds in picturesque mountain scenery.[2]

The Roanoke Red Sulphur Springs was a famous resort, in part due to its
proximity to the Virginia and Tennessee Railroad's depot at Salem. Guests
flocked from all over the country—particularly from the Deep South,
where summer epidemics were greatly feared. Whole families with reti-
nues of servants came to spend the summer—to take the waters and es-
cape unhealthy climates. Southern society patronized resorts such as
Roanoke Red Sulphur both before and after the Civil War.

There were three springs in Roanoke County in the nineteenth century:
Lake Spring at Salem, Botetourt Springs (also known as Johnson's) at Hol-
lins, and Roanoke Red Sulphur Springs. The latter was the most popular,
if contemporary description may be believed. It was first developed by
Capt. Abraham Hupp (1818–62) of Salem.[3] On February 16, 1856, the
Virginia Assembly chartered the Red Sulphur Springs Company after
Hupp and a group of Salem businessmen purchased the grounds around
the Roanoke Red Sulphur Springs. They built a large hotel and cottages.

> This is one of the new places of valetudinary and plea-
> sure resorts which the recent ardor for spring im-
> provement has brought to the public view.
>
> The property is owned by a company of public spir-
> ited gentlemen residing in Roanoke, who with com-
> mendable energy and taste, have within the last three
> years erected the buildings.[4]

After declining patronage during the Civil War years, the resort was taken
over in 1876 by Flavius Josephus Chapman (1839–90), who also operated
the hotel at Lake Spring in Salem. As the vogue for spas died out in the
late nineteenth century, the Roanoke Red Sulphur Springs buildings and
1200-acre site fell into disuse. In 1909 the property was purchased by the
state of Virginia for a sanitorium to treat tuberculosis. By 1937 the old
hotel quartered the staff of Catawba Sanitorium.

During the height of its popularity and prosperity, Roanoke Red Sulphur Springs provided accommodation for as many as three hundred

guests in the hotel and cottages. Called Red Sulphur because of the color of its metallic deposits, the water was described in 1873 as mild and pleasantly sulphurous.[5] In the nineteenth century mineral water was considered beneficial, particularly for those afflicted with lung diseases. In 1882 the Norfolk and Western Railway advertised Roanoke Red Sulphur Springs in a pamplet[6] (see figs. 60, 61), describing the springs in a combination of nineteenth century prose and medical terminology. The advertisement claimed that the grounds lay 2,000 feet above sea level and that there were no fogs or dampness. "The pure, fresh and invigorating air from the mountain heights, the high and dry location of the Springs are highly appreciated by those desiring a change for purpose of health, novelty, recreation and to get rid of the wearing activities of business life. Ample arrangements for all ordinary amusements."[7] The pamphlet advertised the resort as having a table with the best local food, a band, daily mail, and good livery service to and from Salem. Board was two dollars a day, ten dollars a week, and thirty dollars a month, with special rates for big parties and families.

The unknown author of the pamphlet wrote descriptions of the quality and the healing properties of the water. He noted that, unlike most sulphur waters, Red Sulphur Springs water increased the volume of the pulse and diminished its frequency. According to him the waters were particularly helpful in curing "pulmonary affections and vascular excitements" and the waters were also diuretic and had "great efficacy in the cure of renal, vesical, and womb affections."[8] The pamphlet included testimonials from doctors. A Dr. John H. Griffin noted the water's importance in curing chest diseases, but it was Dr. J. J. Moorman, author of a number of books on springs of America and quoted in the Norfolk and Western Railway's pamphlet, who testified to the importance of the waters for curing what today would be called "social" diseases. According to him the Roanoke Red Sulphur Springs water had general effects upon the organs and tissues of a diseased body. "In womb affections and diseases of genito urinary organs of both sexes, dyspepsia, neuralgia, debility supervening upon acute diseases, especially febrile affections, chronic intermittents, chronic rheumatism, gout, and dropsy, the cahexia of scrofula, syphilis and mercury, and some of the diseases of the skin and bone. I believe the water, judiciously employed, would prove eminently beneficial."[9] The water was bottled and sold. Two kinds were offered: "Roanoke Red Sulphur" and "Catawba Iron: All Healing." Both cost four dollars a case; the water was advertised widely for its great curative power.

The fashionable watering resorts that grew up around Virginia's mineral springs were earlier pictured and described by the German artist Edward

Beyer (1820–65), who came to America about 1848. His *Album of Virginia* contains forty lithographs of resorts and other natural attractions in the area. Beyer spent three years working on the drawings and then returned to Germany in 1856 or 1857. Plates made in Dresden and Berlin from these drawings were sent back to Virginia. The album was copyrighted in Richmond in 1858.[10] Beyer's views of resorts such as Roanoke Red Sulphur Springs (fig. 59) show many details of buildings, transportation modes, and costumes. Of the many buildings shown in his view of the Roanoke Red Sulphur Springs, however, only the gazebo and one hotel building remain.

59
**Edward Beyer print: Roanoke
Red Sulphur Springs**
The Album of Virginia, 1857
(Hand-colored lithograph)

Spring Resort Buildings
Roanoke Red Sulphur Springs
Norfolk and Western Railroad
pamphlet
1882

This page is reproduced from *Tourists and Excursionists Guide Book: Summer Homes,* published to entice visitors to the Roanoke area. The three-story hotel and its cottages surround the spring. The wood engraving was copied from an 1857 lithograph by Edward Beyer (fig. 59).

F. J. CHAPMAM, Proprietor.

J. W. WOODS, Gen. Manager.   **L. W. WISE,** Cashier & Clerk.
Mrs. BELLE JORDAN, of Christiansburg, Eating & Linen Dep't.

Will be Open for Visitors May 1, 1882.

The attention of the public is invited to the **advantages and attractions** of this watering place, which has, for a number of years, been so favorably known both for its **curative virtues** and its pleasant and healthful surroundings

AS A DELIGHTFUL SUMMER RESORT!

61
Spring Resort Buildings
Roanoke Red Sulphur Springs
Norfolk and Western Railroad
pamphlet (detail)
1882

This enlarged section from the wood engraving (fig. 60) advertising the Roanoke Red Sulphur Springs shows the two structures that remain today from the resort complex.

62
Monterey
Tinker Creek Lane N.E., Roanoke City
c. 1845
National Register 1974

An unusual example of the Greek Revival is found at Monterey. Built in the 1840s in a rural setting, the house and land remain relatively unchanged today. Giving the illusion of a one-story house with large windows and gracious porches, Monterey typifies the Greek Revival architecture found in the Gulf Coast states. This form of cottage is common in Louisiana and on the Gulf Coast in Mississippi. The low pyramidal roof and hexastyle portico with Doric cornice are unusual in the Valley of Virginia, however.

High ceilings and a wide center hall, now blocked off, also contribute to Monterey's raised-cottage character. The slope of the land enables the house to be two stories high. A veranda goes across the entire front, and there is a two-story gallery at the rear and on a side of the ell. The building is constructed of brick laid in Flemish bond on the front and in American, or common, bond on the other walls. The mortar was painted with a thin white line. This combination of bonds abounds on nineteenth-century buildings in the Roanoke Valley and all over the country. The fancier, more-difficult-to-lay Flemish bond is used on the front for effect, and the simpler, easier-to-lay American is reserved for the sides.

The front veranda is raised and consists of six square columns and two pilasters. As in the Louisiana and Mississippi prototypes, the roof incorporates the porch. Painted blue,[1] the ceiling of the porch has a surrounding entablature. Turned, Victorian-style posts with incised brackets support the upper-level gallery in the back section of the ell. Plate 28 from *The Practical House Carpenter* by Asher Benjamin (Boston, 1830) probably provided the basic plan for the main entrance. The rectangular two-panel door has a glass transom and sidelights hinged for ventilation, another southern feature (see fig. 64). Fluted trim with round corner blocks frame the door transom and sidelights. Doric pilasters with a Greek fret supporting a simple entablature flank the whole design. The two front windows have triple-hung sash, eight-over-eight-over-eight. Two-section louvered blinds hang at all the windows, which are constructed with plain lintels and corner blocks. Standing-seam sheet metal covers Monterey's low hip roof. A Greek Doric cornice with projecting mutules crowns the eaves of the front and sides. Inside, the front door opens into a hall that, for ventilation, originally ran unobstructed from front to back.

Despite its name, the Greek Revival revived both ancient Greek and Roman styles. In the early nineteenth century, the new American republic searched for architectural forms to provide it with a sense of identity. America came of age during that period, and its architecture proclaimed the new democracy in the classical manner. The use of classical orders on the porticoes of residences and government buildings provides the most distinctive feature for the layman to recognize but cornices, architraves, and whole entablatures are often combined with pilasters and columns. Greek and Roman decorative motifs spread widely by the mid-nineteenth century. For residential architecture the details were made of wood. Steam-powered tools and mechanized milling techniques came into use. The Greek Revival is a carpenter's style; widely circulated handbooks allowed even rural communities to keep up with, and to create, the latest in classical architectural fashions. The do-it-yourself manuals showed diagrams for everything: truss forms, spiral staircases, designs for mantel pieces, window and door frames, and many decorative motifs to be used as the carpenter, builder, or customer desired. Even floor plans and elevations were included.

Without a doubt the most popular American handbooks in the Greek Revival manner were those by Massachusetts-born Asher Benjamin (1773–1845). His *American Builder's Companion*, first published in 1830, went through numerous editions, and his even more popular *Practical House Carpenter* had fourteen editions between 1830 and 1857. These and many other handbooks spread Greek Revival forms rapidly throughout the country. Everyone learned the language, but local dialects sprang up also. In the early nineteenth century in rural areas, such as the Roanoke Valley, architecture in the Greek Revival mode, both public and private, was the work of local builders and craftsmen who were loosely adapting designs from such handbooks.

Monterey was built in 1846, as indicated by the $6,000 added to the value of the property owned by Charles Oliver in that year.[2] This was an extraordinarily high evaluation for the time. The inventory and appraisement of his estate, dated October 26, 1853,[3] recorded that he had thirty-four slaves and twenty-one horses, more than usual for the area. Persistent local legend recalled Charles and his son, Yelverton, bringing back the idea for a Gulf Coast–form house after they had raced horses in New Orleans. Charles died sometime before July 1, 1851,[4] and his son, Yelverton, continued living at the plantation amidst furnishings that can only be described as splendid for that time in this area. Yelverton's extensive personal property was inventoried and appraised after his death and was then recorded on July 10, 1857.[5] Whereas most people in the Roanoke Valley lived in simple I houses, or in log cabins, Yelverton Oliver's inventory, which follows, indicates sophisticated tastes, which are also evident in the unusual design of the house his father built.

The Oliver genealogy has been confusing to local historians. Charles Oliver had a son, Yelverton N., who in turn had three children: Charles, Rosaltha, and Yelverton N. (Jr.). The younger son—Y.N., as he was often called—later served in the Confederate army but he was too young, of course, to have been involved in the construction of this house.[6]

July 10, 1857

Inventory and appraisement of household property of
Y. N. Oliver, deceased:

Furniture

Parlour: 2 sofas, 12 chairs, 2 armchairs,
    1 rocking chair $125.00
2 paintings, 4 candle sticks, 3 candle [*illegible*] 50.00

2 glass vases	20.00
2 tables	10.00
3 flower pots and 2 spittoons	2.50
1 clock	5.00
carpet $25 curtains $25	50.00
Brass andirons, shovel and tongs	6.50

Chambers

6 bedsteads and bedding	152.50
2 glass vases	10.00
1 mahogany bureau	20.00
1 washstand and 2 bronze candlesticks	3.50
curtains and matting and andirons	10.00
carpet and mats	2.50
1 sideboard	20.00
2 settees	10.00
1 doz. maple chairs	15.00
6 engravings	3.00
1 lounge	5.00
1 walnut desk $15 and 1 mahogany washstand	30.00
1 mahogany wardrobe, 1 pine wardrobe	55.00
1 glass candle shade	1.50
carpet and curtains	10.00
1 pair fine [*illegible*]	1.00
3 engravings	1.00
1 pair andirons	1.00
2 pine tables	1.00
1 looking glass, carpet and curtains	3.00
1 mahogany bureau	10.00
carpet, andirons, shovel and tongs	2.50
1 looking glass, 1 workstand	8.00
2 pine bedsteads, 2 looking glass, 1 candle-stand	[no price]
2 pine tables, curtains, shovel	[no price]
22 chairs	12.00
1 dining table $25 1 doz. chairs $6	31.00
2 pine tables	.75
1 set castors	20.00
1 Albator tea set	30.00
2 silver salt stands, 1 silver mustard pot	6.00
Glassware	15.00
2 china fruit stands	1.50

1 broken tea set	5.00
1 doz. knives	7.50
1 broken dinner set	15.00
water and coffee pots	7.00
pitchers	7.50
1 pair andirons, shovel and tongs	2.00
pots $5, ovens—$4, 2 bakers $2, 5 gridirons $2	13.00
1 brass kettle $3, 2 pans $.37, 2 trays $1	4.37
3 [*illegible*] cans $1.50, 1 safe $1.50, 4 bowls and pitchers	7.00
tinware	1.50
1 double barrel shotgun	40.00
2 pair pistols, 1 knife	30.00
1 fishing rod	10.00
1 gold watch	100.00
1 metallic barometer	5.00
9 pair cotton sheets, 4 pr. linen sheets	17.00
5 pair linen and 5 pair cotton pillowcases	3.00
7½ pair of blankets	37.00
4 yarn bed covers	20.00
8 white counterpanes	32.00
5 comforters	7.50
6 valences and canopies	9.00
28 towels [*illegible*], 1 doz. napkins $1, 9 table cloths .18	25.75
Mats for dining table	1.50
1 bay horse John	100.00
1 buggy and harness	175.00
1 lot of books	30.00
1 large map	2.50
2 pair decanters	3.10
4 Fancy colored glasses	5.00
1 doz. silver forks, 2 doz. silver spoons	125.00
1 doz. German silver forks	1.25
bottles and demijohns	12.50
1 [*illegible*] case	.75
1 tin [*illegible*]	3.00
1 gold pencil	10.00
1 Mahogany case	2.00

63
Monterey (detail)
Tinker Creek Lane N.E.
Roanoke City
c. 1845

Fireplaces in Monterey are very simple. The forms of the woodwork were loosely derived from Asher Benjamin designs, but no precise correspondences are seen.

64
Monterey (detail)
Tinker Creek Lane N.E.
Roanoke City
c. 1845

Greek Revival millwork surrounds the transoms of the parlors at Monterey. The distinctive "ear" at the top corners is typical of Greek Revival decoration all over the country. The transom opens on hinges at the side to allow maximum ventilation.

65
Belle Aire
1320 Belle Aire Circle S.W., Roanoke City
1849
National Register 1975

A large, two-story, L-shaped house, Belle Aire reflects the Greek Revival style as typically applied in the Roanoke Valley. It is built of brick, using a variety of bonds. The south wall displays a fine early example of all-stretcher bond. Two-story-high stucco Doric pilasters stand at the corners of the building; the original metal drainspouts with applied diamond ornaments sit atop them. The front facade has a two-level pedimented portico, a common form in the South. There are four fluted Doric columns at each level, and as usual, those on the second floor are more delicate than those on the first floor. The west wall is laid in Flemish bond and has corner pilasters and window lintels similar to those on the south facade.

The other walls are made of four- and five-course American bond. A full entablature goes around the eaves of the low hipped roof; there are three interior chimneys.

All the components of Belle Aire's L-plan were built as one integral unit: center hall, one formal parlor on either side, dining room behind one parlor (separated from the main block by a small passage), and stair. The plan represents a more sophisticated space disposition than the I, although the two front rooms and center hall have the same arrangement as the normal Valley of Virginia I. The large rear projection making the L provided space for a dining room or ballroom below and more bedrooms above.

The house was built in 1849 by Madison Pitzer (1799–1861), who had a great deal of land between Salem and Roanoke. An increase of $6,000 in the total value of Madison Pitzer's land and buildings in 1850 indicates that the house was built in the previous year.[1] While the architect and the builder of this house are not known, Gustavus Sedon's journal records that he installed windows here. In 1855 Sedon put in "14 light of window" and charged seventy-five cents for the job.[2]

66
Belle Aire (detail)
1320 Belle Aire Circle S.W.
Roanoke City
1849
Greek Revival woodwork was produced in local mills and installed by local carpenters. The molding and "ear" directly surrounding the tiles on this fireplace were mass-produced. The column was hand carved by an unknown craftsman. The transfer-print tiles are a later addition.

67
Salem Presbyterian Church
East Main Street and Market Street, Salem
1851–52
National Register 1974

In a group of distinctive Greek Revival churches in Southwest Virginia, Salem Presbyterian Church has special significance. The group includes the Methodist, Episcopal, and Presbyterian churches in Fincastle (the

Presbyterian Church was remodeled to its present form), Floyd Presbyterian Church, Bedford Presbyterian, Christiansburg Presbyterian, and the former Methodist Church in Bedford. All these buildings show the Greek Revival style as used by builders in relatively remote areas. Although the Greek Revival details have been changed and simplified, the most common characteristics of this group of churches include the temple form, porticoes in antis, square belfries, and paired pilasters.

The temple form of Salem Presbyterian Church has an Ionic portico in antis. Measuring forty feet by eighty feet, the original building is made of brick laid in a five-course common bond with Flemish variation. The portico at the sides of the doorcases helped to preserve the well-painted white lines on the mortar joints (see Fig. 68), so the church's porch is one of the best places in the Roanoke area to see nineteenth-century brickwork with its various colors, uneven surfaces from inconsistent forming and firing, and careful mortar joints and pointing. Paneled Doric pilasters below an Ionic entablature frame both the front and the sides of this brick building. Molded trim with corner blocks surrounds tall windows. Above each window is a lintel decorated with a Greek fret in the manner of Asher Benjamin (see fig. 73). The frames and details were copied for windows on two additions to the church.

Above the Greek Revival pediment is a belfry with a paneled base and distinctively scrolled consoles at either side. Above the console level, below the twentieth-century cupola, the tower is much cruder in design and workmanship than the rest of the building; the consoles appear to be out of scale. The middle portion of the tower is square, with paired Doric pilasters framing the opening on each side. Originally, a spire was designed for the center section. Edward Beyer's 1857–58 painting of the City of Salem (fig. 69) shows a tall, thin spire at the place where the church is located, although, unfortunately, other, intervening structures prevented his depicting the rest of the building. A letter written in 1866 that describes the scene in the Beyer painting notes "the tall white steeple towards the left of the picture belongs to the Presbyterian Church. . . ."[1] In 1866 the side galleries were removed and the high pulpit was lowered, while the north end of the sanctuary was extended about twenty feet. In 1885–86, due to structural weakening, the clock and steeple were replaced by a mansard roof on the belfry. In 1914 a rear addition perpendicular to the original structure was added to the north end. In 1928 an octagonal dome cupola in the Colonial Revival manner replaced the mansard roof.[2]

Distinctive detailing surrounds three doors on the church's porch. Two on either side, leading to the stair halls, fall in the Greek Revival category, with fret and corner block decorations similar to and in scale with the windows. The center doorcase surrounding double doors with panel trim, on the other hand, shows a very different character (fig. 70). Larger than the other two, it overscales them with heavy forms. This doorcase, and the Ionic columns in front of it perhaps were the work of Gustavus Sedon (see Pleasant Grove). Sedon's early, documented work at Pleasant Grove has Ionic columns and an ornate door case. A Germanic character to Sedon's design shows up in his documented work not only at Pleasant Grove but at Speedwell and at Hollins College. The curvilinear forms and the heavy paneled effect on the Salem Presbyterian Church center door—a Gothic arch used as an antefix at the ends of the design—indicate a rural, maybe Germanic, interpretation of Greek Revival forms. The center antefix has stiff, regular curves that are also reminiscent of Sedon's work. A tale, copied and recopied in the church's records, relates that Mr. Sedon went into the woods, selected and cut a tree, and sawed it into blocks. From two of these blocks he carved Ionic capitals for the columns.[3] Therefore, Gustavus Sedon may have been responsible for the columns and the center doorcase. According to church records, dedication services for the building were held on August 8, 1852, with all of the $4,500 cost paid prior to the dedication.[4] The building serves as Salem's main Presbyterian church and today is an important landmark for the city.

68
Salem Presbyterian Church (detail)
East Main Street and Market Street, Salem
1851–52

The painted line over the mortar joints on the fine brickwork of Salem Presbyterian Church has been protected under the porch since the brick was laid. Many of the best brick buildings of the nineteenth century had this painted-mortar treatment to disguise sloppy workmanship, to make the building look more refined, and to add a note of sophistication. Nineteenth-century taste did not object to imitation of fancier techniques. Painted joints, marbleizing, graining, and other imitations were very common. The lines here are an unusually good survival.

69

Edward Beyer
Salem, Virginia, **oil painting on
canvas (detail)
1857–58**

The original spire of the Salem
Presbyterian Church is de-
picted by Edward Beyer from
his vantage point in what is now
East Hill Cemetery. Unfortunately, the artist could not render the entire building because
of his perspective.

**Salem Presbyterian Church
(detail)
East Main Street and Market
Street, Salem
1851–52**

The door and doorcase of Salem Presbyterian Church bear a resemblance to plate 29 in Asher Benjamin's *Practice of Architecture* (1833) (fig. 71). The carpenter-builder (perhaps Gustavus Sedon) may have seen this plate, or a doorway adapted from it. The similarities between the design and the actual doorway are enough to postulate this relationship. As did many carpenter-builders far away from major style sources in large cities, local builders simplified and adapted the prevailing styles to their own abilities and to the tastes of their patrons.

71
Practice of Architecture
**by Asher Benjamin
(Boston, 1833)
Plate 29**

72

**Salem Presbyterian Church
(detail)
East Main Street and
Market Street, Salem
1851–52**

Greek Revival details such as this window lintel were made popular by the spread of architectural handbooks throughout America. The design for this window, which may have been done by Gustavus Sedon, appears to have been adapted from plate 31 (fig. 73) in *The Practical House Carpenter* by Asher Benjamin (Boston, 1830). Perhaps millwork was used to construct these fashionable details.

73

The Practical House Carpenter
**by Asher Benjamin
(Boston, 1830)
Plate 31**

74
Williams-Brown House-Store
523 East Main Street, Salem
1845–52
National Register 1971

One of the most important commercial buildings remaining in Southwest Virginia is the house-store on Salem's Main Street. This L-shaped brick building stands two and a half stories high with a gable roof of medium pitch. The structure is about thirty-six feet wide, with three bays on the first floor and five on the second. A two-story, one-bay projection from the northeast rear creates the L. Vertical saw marks on the beams in both parts of the basement indicate that an early-nineteenth-century vertical saw was used to cut all these beams.

Several alterations and additions of the late nineteenth and early twentieth centuries have not changed the external character of the building, and the many interior additions and changes of partitions, stairs, walls, and internal doors left the basic plan intact. The front room on the first floor, containing a fireplace at each end, was originally a large rectangular space used for business. There was a small room in the back, with another fireplace. The second floor also contained a front room and a smaller rear room. The second floor opened out onto a porch with enclosed sides. The third floor originally had the same plan as the second. A staircase located between the front and the back rooms served as the only internal vertical passage; there was no central stair-hall originally. Four wooden additions of indeterminate date are still on the back of the house; in 1900 a sleeping porch was built off the east wall.

Many interesting wooden details exist in the building. The little third-floor room retains its original horizontal beaded paneling covering floor and ceiling—with the exception of the window wall, which is plastered. The second floor front contains the original, wooden, double-hung nine-over-six lights with thin muntins. The windows on the first floor have been replaced in the twentieth century. Inside, a few original mantels, moldings, and chair rails remain, and many of the doors made of thin paneled wood joined by mortise and tenon with wooden pegs are still in place.

The most distinctive feature of the house-store is its two-level gallery, formed by an extension of the side walls of the house as an integral part of the structure. The present flooring of the first-floor porch is not the original, because the pattern of later-nineteenth-century circular saw marks on the joists that support it differs from the vertical saw marks on earlier joists. The sawn-work balustrade on the first-floor level is late nineteenth century, but that on the second-floor level appears to be original. The eight simple posts with chamfered edges ending with lamb's-tongues supporting the galleries are probably original. The second-floor porch ceiling is made of wide boards with beaded edges similar to the boards forming paneling in the little attic room.

Resting on a brick foundation, the house-store is built of brick laid in Flemish bond on the front and in common bond on the sides and rear. Traces of the original white paint on the mortar joints still exist in protected places under the gallery ceilings. Three brick chimneys, two on either side of the main body of the house and one on the back, stand flush with the exterior walls. Distinctive arched openings at either end of the first-floor porch give access to the main entrance. Lintels over the windows are unusual. Twelve are plain, but the six front windows and the two side windows over the arched entrances are decorated by recessed bricks laid horizontally above the openings. Mortar, which was originally scored and painted to imitate bricks or stones laid vertically, fills the recess (see fig. 77). Above the arches this treatment gives the appearance of a series of brick voussoirs. Above the rectangular windows the forms are treated in the same way.

The house-store is located on Main Street in Salem, once a major route to Tennessee and Kentucky. An oil painting, executed in 1857 or 1858 by the German artist Edward Beyer, portrays well the house-store's placement in early Salem. The picture was painted from a vantage point looking west from what is now East Hill Cemetery (fig. 77). Beyer shows the town in remarkable detail, and the house-store receives prominent treatment because of the view he chose. Completely finished, the L-shaped house-store has no visible attachments. Its distinctive arches, lintel decorations, and a little sign are shown in the original painting. There is no balustrade on the first floor; people are walking directly into the building from the street (fig. 76).

Beyer painted the scene just after the original owner and builder, William C. Williams, had died in 1852, and while his estate was being settled. According to McCauley's history of Roanoke County,[1] William C. Williams was born in England in 1775 and emigrated to Norfolk, Virginia, with his parents at an unknown date. After his parents died, he became a carpenter's apprentice. He moved to Salem and in 1814 married Margaret Bryan; they had fourteen children. Williams was an active member of the Salem community. Politician, publican, postmaster, and noted promoter of Salem development, he "was the owner of a tract lying adjacent to the town of Salem and several valuable houses and lots in the town of Salem."[2]

Despite these other activities Williams was primarily a contractor and had many commissions in the Salem area. He built residences for Joshua R. C. Brown, Sr., and Z. Boon, but his main work was the Roanoke County Courthouse. "In entering into the contract for building the Courthouse he looked more to the public good than to his own private interests, for he undertook the work believing it would prove a financial loss, and the event justified his belief."[3] Formed in 1838 from Botetourt County, Roanoke County needed a court facility, and especially a jail. An agreement dated August 24, 1838, between the new county commissioners, Linsay Shoemaker and William C. Williams, read that they would erect public buildings, "namely a Court House and Jail for the sum of $10,400."[4] Williams must have been experienced enough in the construction business—with adequate capital, access to supplies, and laborers—to execute this commission.

In August 1852 Williams died.[5] One of his fourteen children, a son named William W., was living in the area. A daughter, Mary J., had married J. R. C. Brown, Jr.[6] On June 21, 1854, J. R. C. Brown, Jr., as administrator of his father-in-law's estate, sold the house-store to William W. Williams. On the same day William W. Williams resold it to J. R. C. Brown, Sr.[7] Williams's complex estate was not settled until 1855. The building subsequently became known as the Brown House-Store and remained in the possession of the Brown family until 1963.

The fact that William C. Williams owned considerable property in and around Salem confuses the house-store's history. A surveyor's report dated March 10, 1845, first mentions a store when it states ". . . from the Brick Store owned by William C. Williams (at the eastern end) along the Main Street. . . ."[8] His 1845 tax assessment[9] shows no tax added for buildings. In 1846, buildings increased his assessment to $2,000. Williams sold some land in 1846, but retained Salem's lot number 58, containing a store, and this lot number and the building are noted in the 1846 tax assessment.[10] The $2,000 tax assessment for buildings on this property remained constant through 1854,[11] two years after Williams's death, despite tearing down and rebuilding on this lot, as indicated by carpenters' bills.

Salem was a growing community in the 1840s and 1850s, and commercial ventures grew and changed. Claims submitted to Williams's estate after his death in August 1852 provide detailed documentation of his construction undertakings. He died intestate; in accordance with Virginia law, claims on his estate had to be submitted to the court. Fortunately, many of the vouchers for these claims still exist.[12] They disclose fascinating information on the work on the house-store, as well as on nineteenth-century construction and renovation techniques.

Two carpenters by the names of Stokes and Pusey, who had been working for William C. Williams, submitted their bill to his estate for payment.[13] Both these men had been supplying materials and providing labor for Williams's various undertakings. Their bill for $1,638.48 consists of six pages written in longhand. An amount of $362.50 was added as interest from "12 May 1852 to 1st August 1855," when the estate was finally settled. The bill details a number of construction projects but fails to identify specific buildings or to indicate anything more than general periods of time when Stokes and Pusey worked. Some items relate to the house-store, but others are impossible to identify.

Stokes and Pusey's bill begins with a notation about drying lumber and proceeds through construction of shelves, doors, and stairs. Numerous entries indicate rebuilding, major renovation, and construction. Attached to this bill is a separate bill itemizing lumber from Bellvue Mills. The mill list includes 1,260 feet of flooring, 250 feet of one-inch plank, 200 feet of weatherboarding, and 2,000 shingles. These items may signify the construction of an additional new building or a major renovation. The mill bill—coupled with Stokes and Pusey's construction of frames, flooring, ceilings, windows, staircases, and platforms—could indicate that the house-store was being built. In a long list dated May 12, 1852, many items that refer to a store appear. Thirty-four feet of shelving and counters, for instance, appear on the list. Other items are grouped under four entries dated 1851. Confusing the issue are two items, again dated May 12, 1852: "Cutting out old wall and sill frame" and "Setting door in old wall." They may indicate renovation of an existing building. The last item on Stokes and Pusey's May 12 bill reads "8 colloms [*sic*] to front porch $10–$80."[14] Eight *posts* occupy the front of the house-store, but perhaps Stokes and Pusey did not differentiate between columns and posts.

Also attached to Stokes and Pusey's bill is a bill from John C. Deaton, a carpenter and laborer, detailing his work for the two carpenters from August 12, 1851, through September 29, 1852. Deaton must have continued to work after William C. Williams died. On August 12, 1851, he "commence[ed] work on the new store house . . . ", and subsequently he worked on this job for $.88 per day. On November 10 of the same year he spent "four days tearing down, cleaning out the old store counter and shelves and porch." This entry hints that there was a previous store. After stopping work on December 15, 1851, Deaton worked again in the spring of 1852 for six days beginning April 5 "in the cellar laying floors, putting up shelves, fixing steps, hanging blinds in the new store." The Deaton bill, with its numerous references to "new store" and "new brick store house," confirms that a building was being completed.[15]

The bill from Deaton to the Williams estate also includes a bill for work done by Charles M. Elam at $.40 per day. Elam was probably the carpenter's assistant. Sometimes the Elam notations refer to an "old" or a "new store-house," but on August 12, 1851, Elam spent four days "work on the brick store house." From September 4 through September 30, 1851, Elam worked for nineteen days, "laying floors in the new store house." In October he worked sixteen and one-half days "on the new store house" without specifying the particular job. Then on November 1 he worked one day "finishing the new store house." Elam's final notation, for November 10, notes "6 days tearing down and cleaning out the old store house." This further evidence points to the finishing of a store-house.[16]

The vouchers submitted after William C. Williams's death do not completely clarify the problem of when the existing house-store was built. On all the vouchers the differences between the workmen's use of the terms *brick store*, *brick store house*, and *new brick store house* is difficult to decipher. Vertical file documents, deed books and landbooks, and the bills submitted to the Williams's estate do not all agree. Imprecise record keeping, poor handwriting and spelling, and lack of consistency in terminology hinder exact dating. The survey of March 10, 1845,[17] does show conclusively that Williams owned a brick store on Main Street of Salem. The bills from Stokes and Pusey and others offer evidence of an old building being torn down and a new structure replacing it.

As completed by Stokes, Pusey, and their helpers, the Williams-Brown House-Store stands as a fine example of mid-nineteenth-century commercial vernacular architecture in Salem. As a rare surviving example of its type, the building was the area's first structure to be placed on the Virginia Landmark Register and the National Register of Historic Places.

75
Williams-Brown House-Store (detail)
523 East Main Street, Salem
1845–52

The decorative lintels and the arches with painted joints to imitate fine stonework may still be seen on the Williams-Brown House-Store. Compare this view showing the raised porch floor with the detail of Edward Beyer's painting showing the same porch in 1857–58 (fig. 76).

76
Edward Beyer
Salem, Virginia, **(oil painting on canvas) (detail)**
1857–58

Still facing Main Street as it was in 1852, when it was built (and between 1857 and 1858 when Edward Beyer painted it—as shown in this detail), the Williams-Brown House-Store has always been one of Salem's most conspicious buildings. Originally patrons went directly into the store from the street.

77
Edward Beyer
Salem, Virginia (oil painting on canvas)
1857–58

Written by William McCauley in a letter dated March 14, 1866, to his brother James is the best description of the Beyer painting and the city of Salem at the time it was done.

Dear Brother James:

I also enclose a picture of Salem as it was in the year 1859. It has undergone considerable change since that time, but the main features as you see them in the picture are unchanged. I judge you would be at some loss to know what was the standpoint of the artist. I will endeavor to explain the main features. The artist (this is a photograph from a very correct painting made in 1857 or 8) was stationed on the hill near the old Baptist Church. The large garden enclosed with the white fence, on the right, you will at once recognize as that of Mr. F. Johnston.

The house back of it, embowered among the trees is his. The first white house on the left with its gable and chimney facing you is Mr. Shirey's where I am now living. Just beyond it and considerably in the shade is the Presbyterian parsonage. These two buildings have been put up since you left in 1849. The low dingy house, the first on the right after passing Mr. J's garden is the well known to you blacksmith shop, in which Mr. Day wielded the hammer for many years. The long white house with the gable towards Main Street is a building put up by Mr. Burwell. It is on the corner of Cove Road and Main Street. Just beyond and across the Cove Road is Mr. Joshua Brown's establishment which will no doubt seem familiar to you. The large building a little to the right of the centre of the picture and setting prominently on a hill was built by Powell Huff, but is now the residence and property of one of the daughters of Col. H. H. Chapman dec'd. It is the most attractive location in Salem. This hill was when you left a cultivated field. It is now dotted with houses for half a mile in the direction of the mountain. The large block of buildings to the right of this is the residence of Hon. A. A. Edmonson. The steeple near the centre of the picture is that of the Methodist Church, located just where the circuses formerly had their rings and pitched their tents. The tall white steeple towards the left of the picture belongs to the Presbyterian Church, having for its site the spot where used to be Jim Huff's battery, adjoining Mr. J. P. Kizer's lot. A little to the right of this in the picture you see the cupola of the Lutheran "College" Church. It is situated on the corner of Main and the cross street leading up by the Jail and Methodist Church. Midway (in the picture) between the Lutheran and Methodist Churches you see peeping out from the trees and roof an upper portion of the Court House. The picture is on too small a scale to show the buildings distinctly.

Affectionately,

Your Brother William

78

Benjamin Deyerle Place (also called Winsmere or Lone Oaks)
1402 Grandin Road Extension S.W., Roanoke City
c. 1853
National Register 1973

Another L-shaped house displays a simple facade with Greek Revival detailing. Its brick bonds stand out—three rows of stretchers alternating with one row of Flemish bond on the sides. The brick bond on the basement level of the front facade consists of Flemish bond every fourth row with common bond between; all rows above the basement level are common bond. A horseshoe-shaped staircase, built in the twentieth century to replace straight wooden steps, leads up to the house's main entrance. The simple pedimented Doric entrance portico has plain square pillars and narrow fluted columns with exaggerated entasis. The doorway is also simple, with paneled pilasters and slender sidelights. Window caps on the first and second stories, with dog-eared wooden lintels, are Greek Revival details. Corner pilasters are an important feature of the design. A heavy entablature goes all the way around the house and masks the low hip roof.

The two front rooms with a center hall resemble the I-form house, but the rear section gives the L-form. A curving staircase leads to the second floor from the center hall. The walls of the upper hall curve with the stairway, as does an upper hall window.

A number of outbuildings remain on the property: quarters, store building, and a small brick building (fig. 21) possibly used as a kiln. The molded brick cornice on this latter outbuilding is particularly fine.

Benjamin Deyerle's brick house was built as his residence prior to 1853 on a tract called Mud Lick. The Roanoke County Land Book for 1853 shows an assessed value of $5,500 for buildings located on his Mud Lick property. In the years immediately preceding, the sum assessed on this property for his mill had been $4,000, but opposite the 1853 entry is written: "$1,500 added for improvements, 1853."[1] (The tax assessor used the word *improvements* to mean additions and new buildings throughout the 1851–55 Land Book.) Using his own slave labor and brick that he furnished himself, Benjamin Deyerle (1806–83) probably built this large house for $1,500. From this home, he operated many commercial ventures as a large-scale farmer, with considerable tracts of land in Roanoke and Franklin counties. He acquired land early in his career for various agricultural endeavors. Census reports of 1850, 1860, and 1870 list him as a farmer. Much of his land was planted in corn, wheat, and tobacco. Other areas were used for grazing cattle and hogs. "Deyerle was a man of diversified interest. He had a large distillery in which much of his grain was turned into whiskey. On one of the streams that flowed through the plantation, he erected a mill for grinding all kinds of grain and also built kilns for burning brick and furnishing brick for many buildings through the country [county]."[2]

Reminiscing in Iowa seven months before his death in December 1934, the Reverend P. M. Lewis—son of Charles Lewis, who had been a slave of Benjamin Deyerle—corresponded with a granddaughter of Benjamin Deyerle, after having been interviewed in the Iowa newspaper. He described his father as "a great distiller of whiskeys and a great brick molder and layer."[3] He further related that his father laid the brick "in front of the house"[4] that is now called Lone Oaks, the house called White Corners (fig. 79), and the home of Benjamin Keagy (fig. 107), as well as "many others in Roanoke, Franklin, and other counties around Roanoke."[5] The brick bond on Lone Oaks and White Corners is the same, but that on the

Keagy house appears to be a variation. Most nineteenth-century brick houses had the best formed and best laid bricks on their front facades. Doubtless, Charles Lewis was Benjamin Deyerle's master bricklayer, who was given the task of laying bricks on the facade of these houses.

Since the early part of the twentieth century, local historians have associated Benjamin Deyerle, as planner or as contractor, for several houses in the Roanoke Valley. No documentary evidence has been found to verify this tradition, however.

79
White Corners
1606 Persinger Road S.W.
Roanoke City
c. 1858

The distinctive corner pilasters seen here are repeated on several houses in the Roanoke Valley. Characteristic of the late Greek Revival style are the heavy entablature, the large windows, and the heavy doorcase. This house has an unusual mixture of brick bondings. The front has American, or common, brick bond; the left side of the house has four rows of stretchers and a fifth of Flemish bond; the right side has a mixture of bonds; and the back has American bond. This house is planned with one room on either side of a center hall—the standard I-form—and an extension to the rear.

80
Intervale
Midland Road, Salem
c. 1854

Similar to Lone Oaks and White Corners with its two-story corner pilasters and heavy entablature, this house has the basic I-form of two rooms and a center hall. Behind, at a right angle, are rooms creating an L-form. The Greek Revival porch has unusual square columns.

81
Pleasant Grove
Route 11 South, Roanoke County: Glenvar
1853

Pleasant Grove was built for Joseph Deyerle (1799–1877), who owned a large tract of land along the Roanoke River. The house is roughly cube-shaped. The plan—a four-over-four of Georgian eighteenth century derivation (fig. 82)—has four rooms, two on either side of the central hall, and there are four chimneys, two on each end of the house, to serve each of the four rooms on each floor. Two inscribed bricks are laid in the right corner of the facade. One brick bears the name "Joseph Deyerle," along with the date "1853," and another brick is also incised with the date "1853." The Roanoke County Land Book of 1854 notes the value of Joseph Deyerle's 125 acres on the Roanoke River as $3,500, a $2,000 increase from the previous year. Opposite the 1854 valuation, a note reads, "$2,000 added for Imp. 1853."[1]

With its distinctive Ionic portico, Pleasant Grove's woodwork is one of the best examples of the carpentry work of Gustavus Sedon.[2] Sedon's career spans the second half of the nineteenth century. When Sedon died in 1893, the Roanoke area had grown from small, isolated farms and villages to a thriving railroad-oriented town. The work of Gustavus Sedon is some of the first documented architectural history uncovered about local building. Sedon undertook small construction jobs, including the building of cabins and outbuildings, but his signature is most obvious on large-scale projects such as his work at Pleasant Grove.

Some of the most complete entries in his journal concern Joseph Deyerle. They log Sedon's carpentry work on the house during the year 1853. Sedon noted that he worked seven months and twenty-four days for Joseph Deyerle and that he was paid $40 per month, for a total of $316.75. The items for which he charged extra provide insight into the creation of architectural details on Pleasant Grove. Amazingly, all of the embellishments made by Sedon and noted in his journal are still in place. He recorded four carved mantelpieces as "4 Caps mantelpeice [sic] carve" (fig. 85) and charged two dollars for all of them. For carving "The beet [bead] cross Housdoor," he also charged two dollars. The highest price of all the items he supplied for the Joseph Deyerle house was for the carved panel now in the front parlor. An open-worked carving, this piece now hangs over a door, but since Sedon called it a window panel, it originally may have been inserted into a window frame to modulate light. The curves of the panel are similar in feeling to those on the Speedwell doorcase (fig. 27) and to the decoration on the ceiling of the rear porch of Main Dormitory at Hollins College.

Sedon must have spent considerable time carving thirty-four feet of what he called "egg molding" around the portico, even though he only charged six dollars. Today this may be seen around the door (fig. 84) and on the Ionic capitals. Sedon also noted that he carved "1 colum cap portiko [sic]" for six dollars, which probably refers to all six Ionic capitals (see fig. 83). The entry may mean column-capped portico. In any case, the porch at Pleasant Grove is one of the finest examples of Greek Revival carving found in the area.

The six beautifully proportioned Ionic columns epitomize Sedon's wood-carving skill. The handsome egg-and-dart molding gives a horizontal emphasis to the portico design. Delicate muntins in the transom and sidelights lend grace to the door's design. The elliptical motif in the transom, similar to that at Speedwell, creates a rhythmical pattern. Gothic arches in the sidelights offer a vertical accent in a horizontal composition, and the Gothic arches in the mullions of the overlight, with Doric pilasters on both sides, help to make the Pleasant Grove entrance one of the finest in Roanoke County.

In later years Sedon did more work for Joseph Deyerle. In 1855, Sedon's journal shows that he installed the iron balustrade, which still adorns the top of the front porch. Obviously, this elaborate cast-iron work was ordered, and Sedon merely put it in place. There is, however, no manufacturer's name on it.[3] Iron balustrades with units of the same pattern are on the Alexander-Withrow House in Lexington, Virginia, and on a house at 2426 Church Street and the Adams House on Cabell Street in Lynchburg, Virginia. The last entry for Joseph Deyerle, in 1868, shows that Sedon rebuilt a grainery and constructed two window frames and blinds for the main door.

Surviving outbuildings at Pleasant Grove include a two-room brick building, a springhouse (fig. 17), and a kitchen, now attached to the main house.

82
Four-over-Four House (plan)
The two-room-deep Georgian plan was an expensive form for a house in this area. The I-form house, half of a Georgian plan, was much more common. The second floor of a four-over-four house has the same plan as the first.

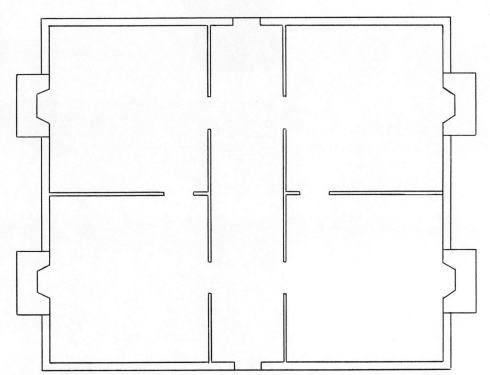

83
Pleasant Grove (detail)
Route 11 South, Roanoke
County: Glenvar
1853

The Ionic columns at Pleasant Grove represent some of the finest Greek Revival detail in the Valley and are markedly similar to these on the front portico of Main Dormitory at Hollins College (fig. 93).

84
Pleasant Grove (detail)
Route 11 South, Roanoke
County: Glenvar
1853

In 1853 Gustavus Sedon charged six dollars for carving thirty-four feet of egg-and-dart molding over the door and sidelights at Pleasant Grove.

85

85

Pleasant Grove (fireplace)
Route 11 South, Roanoke
County: Glenvar
1853

In 1853 Gustavus Sedon carved Ionic pilasters on the fireplace in the front parlor of Pleasant Grove. Joseph Deyerle, who commissioned the carving, paid Sedon fifty cents for this work.

86

Four-over-Four House
6103 Plantation Road, Roanoke
County
c. 1860

Houses built following a two-room-deep Georgian plan are unusual in this part of Virginia—where the I-plan was prevalent. Here brick is laid in Flemish bond on the front and in American bond on the sides. The porch has been substantially changed, but the original carved window lintels are still in place.

93

87
Buena Vista
Penmar Avenue and Ninth Street S.E., Roanoke City
1850 and 1892
National Register 1974

Reflecting the Valley's nineteenth-century prosperity, Buena Vista is a
good example of a Greek Revival country residence. Local builders, using
local labor, probably erected the structure. The house consists of two dis-
tinct and somewhat strangely connected buildings. Each section was built
at a different time with no attempt to integrate the roof lines of the two
buildings where they meet in an awkward junction. A little wooden corridor connection on the second floor was added sometime in the late nineteenth century.

The main section is a two-story rectangle, with a smaller, connected
two-story building; a one-story wing built in 1962 juts out at the rear of

the main section. Massive and imposing, with a two-story distyle Greek Doric portico dominating the facade, the main section contains two interior end chimneys. Simple Doric pilasters and an entablature surround the sidelights and transom at the main door. The main house has a central-hall plan on the first and second floors; sliding doors separate the two rooms on each side of the hall. A shallow hip roof covers the structure. At Buena Vista the brick facade of the main building has bricks of high quality and a deep red color, but they were laid with the simplest technique—all stretchers, except for one row of headers at the foundation level. On the east side, American bond was used, while Flemish bond was employed on the west side. (Normally, the Flemish bond, in high-quality brickwork, would appear on the front.) The bricks of the smaller building were laid in American bond with a water table. This section also has Doric pilasters, but they are smaller in proportion and paired at the corners.

William Langhorne, father-in-law of George P. Tayloe, first appears in the records in 1823, when he bought 598 acres of property on the Roanoke River.[1] In 1824, the first year William Langhorne was assessed, $600 was the "sum added on account of buildings."[2] Two years later, in 1826, William Langhorne was assessed $1,000 "for improvement," according to the tax record's "Explanation of alterations during the preceding year."[3] The assessed value for buildings remained constant, despite Tayloe's purchase of 120 acres of the property in 1833 from his father-in-law.[4]

Tayloe was born at Mount Airy Plantation in Richmond County. He grew up in the famous Octagon House in Washington. After graduation from Princeton, he married Langhorne's daughter in 1830. They moved to the Roanoke area, where he managed two iron furnaces. Adding to his property, he acquired more than 500 acres on the Roanoke River including the house that had been built by his father-in-law. Although this part of Botetourt County became Roanoke County in 1838, for some reason Tayloe's deed to the property was not recorded in Roanoke County until August 31, 1845.[5] The taxes are recorded in Roanoke County under Langhorne's name until 1847, when Tayloe is listed with $2,000 added on "account of buildings."[6] The Roanoke County assessors had doubled the value of the buildings in their reassessment of 1840.[7] In 1848 and 1849 the assessed value of buildings remained the same.

In 1850 an additional assessment of $8,000 records "the new Buildings is [*sic*] included."[8] This notation shows that Tayloe completed an expensive building on his property sometime just prior to the 1850 assessment. The larger house, with its four-over-four plan—so typical of the nineteenth century mansions in nearby Botetourt County—would have been the height of fashion in 1850. In fact, Buena Vista was one of the noteworthy mansions of its time, as described by a visitor to the area in 1862: ". . . spacious, peace-embowered home, nestled close to the river, under the looming Mill Mountain, whose afternoon shadows were already creeping across the lawn of oaks and elms, and maples and hickories, with the summer breezes stealing around its white pillars and through its wide hallways and swaying its muslin curtains."[9]

From his imposing home, George P. Tayloe went out into his community and state to become one of the founders of Hollins College, a member of the Virginia General Assembly, and a delegate to the Secession Convention of 1861. The small section of his home attached to the large Greek Revival house was probably finished in 1892. Some evidence for this date may be found by comparing the saw marks on the basement and first-floor joists of the larger house with saw marks on corresponding joists supporting the smaller house. The saw marks on the floor joists of the larger house are vertical indicating the use of a vertical saw blade—probably powered by water or steam—while the saw marks on the floor joists of the smaller house are semicircular, indicating the use of a circular saw blade. The circular saw blade came into common use in the latter part of the nineteenth century, and evidence of this technology is critical to the late date of the smaller house. Two brick walls of the smaller house abut the completed brick wall of the larger house, further indicating that the smaller section was added onto the completed larger house. In addition, landbook records of tax-assessment changes show that between 1892 and 1893, $6,500 was added to the assessment of M. M. Rogers[10] (son-in-law of George P. Tayloe), who had received the property in 1890.[11] The extra assessment and the technological evidence point to the construction of the small house and probably a restoration of the big house in 1892–93. Changed window sashes and Colonial Revival woodwork in the big house probably date from this time also.

George P. Tayloe died in 1897, but the property remained in his family until 1937, when his descendants sold the house and property to the city of Roanoke. Today the building is maintained as the Southeast Recreation Center in Jackson Park.

88
Hollins College Quadrangle
Route 11, Roanoke County: Hollins
1856–1901
National Register 1974

The Hollins College Quadrangle with its red brick buildings accented with white wood reveals the history of the college and its growth, as well as shows the development of nineteenth- and early-twentieth-century collegiate architecture. Buildings, lawns, and walkways shaded by ash, elm, and sugar maple trees enhance the quadrangle's peaceful atmosphere. Each building is noteworthy in itself and contributes to an interesting architectural complex. A tremendous copper beech tree growing between Cocke Memorial Building and East Dormitory and the other trees in the quadrangle preserve the unique atmosphere of Hollins College.

97

89
West Dormitory
Hollins College
Center: 1901; Wings: 1890 (picture c. 1901)

Hollins College began by utilizing the Botetourt Springs Hotel, which was built about 1820. In the late nineteenth century, money was not available to demolish the old hotel, so wings were added in 1890. In 1900, the old hotel was replaced by the present three-story structure, which filled in the space between the brick wings. It was designed by Roanoke architect H. H. Huggins, who advertised in a 1900 directory for the city of Roanoke: "Hollins Institute's fine new building by me. You ought to see this building when finished."[1] In 1901 Hollins paid H. H. Huggins on June 2, August 30, and November 26 a total of $688.70. Payments are listed in a ledger,[2] which has pasted in the back cover a sheet titled "New Building," listing names and totals. "Huggins" is listed with a total of $688.70 beside his name. Constructed by Lewton and Kirkbride, contractors from Roanoke, the structure was completed in 1900.[3] The new center portion had a pedimented pavilion with a projecting portico set on a brick arcade. The portico on the second-floor level had pairs of Doric columns placed on pedestals, with an entablature and balustrade above. Below the portico on either side of the brick arcade, first-story wooden galleries with bracketed posts extended across the wing area. Gable fronts distinguish the old wings. Since the 1900 reconstruction, the three sections of West Dormitory merge harmoniously, and the whole composition appears as a single building.

90
East Dormitory
Hollins College
1856–58

Considered to be the most architecturally significant building on the Hollins campus, East Dormitory—built between 1856 and 1858[1]—is a three-story Greek Revival structure of brick. An impressive three-tiered portico fronts the building. Fluted Greek Doric columns set on one-story-high round piers rise two stories. A Doric entablature crowns the facade. East Dormitory's distinctive Classical Revival architecture has been described by Frances Niederer.

> In East Building appear both Greek and Roman Revival elements. Properly Greek are the Doric columns, their tapered shafts with twenty flutes meeting the three annulets under the well-proportioned capitals. Greek too are the frieze, with its square metopes and triglyphs that meet at the corners, and the inclined mutules under the cornice. But the narrow architrave above the capitals is Roman, as is the splayed profile of the guttae. These little pegs are absent from the mutules, although the holes for them are aligned in the proper Greek fashion.[2]

Balconies shade the second- and third-story levels. Double glass paneled doors open onto the balconies from each floor. The center door on the second-floor balcony has a large rectangular transom and sidelights. East Building is divided vertically into three sections; the only means of reaching another section on the same floor is via the balconies. Originally the ground floor contained lecture rooms and an office.

According to the March 5, 1856, minutes of the Board of Trustees of Hollins Institute, the Building Committee reported that it would be feasible to build "a block of buildings similar to the one we now occupy [The Botetourt Springs Hotel]."[3] On July 4 of that same year, the board met and made plans to alter the portico of the new building at a cost not to exceed $300. They were doubtlessly adding more Classical Revival decoration, which would have been fashionable in 1856 in this area. D. C. Yates was the contractor, but O. W. Brown directed the brickwork.[4]

East Dormitory, an outstanding example of the Classical Revival for Roanoke County, stands today remarkably unchanged. Frances Niederer notes the similarity of East Dormitory—in fact, of the whole Hollins Quadrangle—to the architecture of springs resorts in southwestern Virginia and West Virginia.[5] The central quadrangle retains the flavor of nineteenth-century resort complexes.

91
East Dormitory (detail)
Hollins College
1856–58

Greek and Roman Revival details were used for the sophisticated decoration on East Dormitory. Doric columns in the Greek manner are contrasted with the architrave in the Roman style.

92
Main Building
Hollins College
1861–79

Main Building is a blend of the Classical Revival and various other nineteenth-century styles. In the center of the structure a pair of Ionic columns resting on an arcaded podium supports a pediment. Scrollwork fills the pediment. The brick bond on the sides is American, with Flemish variation, and there is common bond on the front and back. The veranda, which stretches across the front of Main Building, is composed of wooden arches, each supported by a pair of wooden posts. In 1879 a cupola and back porch were added, but, the cupola was taken down after the turn of the century. The back porch is similar in form to the front veranda. Until 1883 the south side of Main Building served as the chapel. From 1870 to 1890, the basement served as the college dining room. In one of the small first-floor rooms is a fireplace mantel that was saved from the parlor of the old Botctourt Springs Hotel. Main Building now houses some offices, lounges, and dormitory rooms.

101

The building of Main was a lengthy process. Contracts were awarded to David Deyerle, brickworker, and Gustavus Sedon, carpenter, in 1860.[1] If an architect designed the building, his name has never surfaced. Construction began April 17, 1861—which was, unfortunately, the day the state of Virginia seceded from the Union. The war made work slow and difficult. Notations about Hollins appear in the journal of Gustavus Sedon from 1855 through 1880.[2] Between 1855 and 1858 Sedon's journal showed a great deal of work at Botetourt Springs for "C. Cocke," who was Charles Lewis Cocke, founder of Hollins College. Sedon made doors, mantelpieces, and window blinds, as well as undertaking major construction for the college. The early journal notations record small items. In August 1855 Sedon was obviously helping Charles Cocke get ready for the opening of a new school year. The journal shows that he made one door, one mantelpiece, and fourteen feet of partitions, and that he repaired other doors and supplied hinges, screens, and miscellaneous hardware.

The Board of Trustees of Hollins gave Sedon a good deal of work just prior to the Civil War, but his work at Hollins was limited during the war. In 1866, work picked up on Hollins' Main Building. Sedon noted that he provided columns for the dining room at a price of $40. His notations of major work continuing on Main provide an invaluable record of construction techniques between 1870 and 1872. The most expensive item recorded shows construction of about 300 feet of porch and two large stairways in 1870. Then in 1871 he installed 196 feet of balustrade, a staircase, three pairs of blinds, and a door. In January 1872 more architectural work for Main Building—eighteen lintels, a gangway, footsteps with handrail, and finally 4,000 shingles—showed that the front exterior of the building was almost finished. In the fall of 1872, Main Building received more work, particularly on the inside. After finishing ten rooms over the chapel for $240, which included the cost of lumber, he installed eight window sashes and completed a floor in a servant's room. He also made two large tables for the dining room. Sedon marked his account settled on July 2, 1873.

The Sedon journal indicates further work on the rear of Main in 1878. Beginning with a series of entries for the month of May and continuing into 1879, Sedon worked primarily at Hollins Institute. He installed eighteen lintels over the back windows and placed two columns under the rear gallery (fig. 94). He also put in a large number of blinds, which he noted in the journal as completed and painted. In 1879, Sedon recorded that he finished the back of Main Building for $175 and the steeple for $200. Main Building was then completed. Today much of Sedon's carpentry work may still be seen.

93
Main Building (detail)
Hollins College
1861–79

The front gable of Main Building has a scroll design inside,
which Gustavus Sedon added
and then recorded in his journal
in 1878. The columns may be
compared with those at Pleasant
Grove (fig. 83).

94
Main Building (detail)
Hollins College
1861–79

A column on the rear porch of
Main Building at Hollins carved
by Gustavus Sedon may be
compared with similar columns
he carved at Speedwell (fig. 83).

95
Bradley Hall
Hollins College
1883

A chapel between Main and East dormitories was the next addition to the Hollins College complex. Breaking with the Classical Revival forms of the other buildings, the chapel, built in 1883,[1] is vaguely Romanesque, overlaid with Roman detail. The front porch and gable display Tuscan capitals. Above the porch is an enlarged dormer with two arched openings. Round-topped windows on the front are set into blind arches. Wooden arcades connect the chapel to the dormitories on both sides, so that it blends with the whole quadrangle. Gustavus Sedon may have worked on the chapel, for there are payments from Hollins College to him in 1883. Sedon, however, did not record specific transactions for this building in his journal. Today the interior contains offices on the ground floor and a recital auditorium on the seond floor.

96
Botetourt Dining Hall
Hollins College
1890

Hollins College built a dining hall in 1890,[1] but did not name it Botetourt Hall until the 1930s. Unconventional in shape and some sixty feet in diameter, it is an outstanding octagonal structure in Virginia, where octagonal buildings seldom appear. The writings of O. S. Fowler, whose *Octagon Mode of Building* was published in 1853, stimulated interest in the octagon form in the mid-nineteenth century. Fowler noted that the octagon was a new way of enclosing public buildings, much better and cheaper than other methods.

Generations of Hollins students ate their meals in the big octagonal dining room, which formed an efficient and grand space for the college for many years. Botetourt Hall is a late manifestation of the octagon phenomenon. The choice of this form was one of numerous architectural innovations at Hollins, and modern additions to the campus carry on this innovative spirit.

Botetourt Hall was built of brick laid in American bond, supplied by C. Nininger for $1,000.[2] Cutout ornamental details embellish the gallery at the top. Two small arched windows, surrounding one wider arched window, pierce each side of the octagon. Inside is a domed central area, and scroll-sawn brackets support each corner of the octagon.

105

97
Roanoke College, Main College Complex
Administration Building (center), Miller Hall (right), Trout Hall (left)
College Avenue, Salem
1848–54, 1857, 1867
National Register 1972

Roanoke College was founded in 1842 as Virginia Collegiate Institute at Mount Tabor in Augusta County, but in 1847 that school moved to Salem. By 1853, the institution was rechartered as a college, with the new name.[1] Today the old campus retains some of its nineteenth century atmosphere, with brick buildings set on expansive lawns shaded by large trees.

The Administration Building, set at the north end of College Avenue, dominates the nineteenth century buildings. It forms an attractive vista from Salem's Main Street. As first built, the Administration Building was a simple brick Greek Revival structure with a three-story center section and two wings. Each wing had a shallow hip roof. The center section had a Doric portico but no pediment, and was surmounted by a domed cupola. Simple stucco pilasters framed the bays in each wing. Originally, the lower floors were meeting halls and classrooms, with dormitory rooms on the upper floors. The college awarded contracts for this center building on May 19, 1847, to James C. Deyerle and Joseph Deyerle for the brickwork. A. M. and T. N. Jordan were hired to do the carpentry. By 1852, the two-story west wing was added, and in 1854 the two-story east wing completed the building.[2]

The present appearance of the Administration Building dates from a 1903 alteration and enlargement in the Neoclassical style. Noah Hockman, a Salem draftsman and builder,[3] drafted the remodeling plans. A third story was put on each of the wings, and a hip roof was then added to cover the entire building. A large Roman Corinthian portico with fluted columns and pediment replaced the original Doric portico. The pediment, Corinthian pilasters, and entablature give the building its present character.

Flanking the Administration Building and set perpendicular to it are two simple, rectangular, three-story brick buildings with pedimented gables. There have been substantial changes in the exterior of Miller Hall, on the right, completed in 1857, while Trout Hall, on the left, retains essentially the appearance it had upon its completion in 1867.

98
Bittle Hall
Roanoke College
College Avenue, Salem
1879
National Register 1972

Another important building at Roanoke College is Bittle Hall, started in 1878, and completed in 1879.[1] According to Eisenberg's history of Roanoke College, a $3,000 contract was given in 1878 to J. C. Deyerle for brickwork, H. W. Hundly for carpentry, and Noah Hockman for unspecified work.[2] In the *Virginia State Business Directory, 1871–72*, "J. C. Deyerle, Salem," is the only brickmaker listed in this area of the state, while "Noah Hockman" is listed under carpenters and builders.[3] By 1884, however, "N. Hockman, Salem," is listed as an architect in the *Virginia Classified Business Directory*, while J. C. Deyerle retains his classification as a brickmaker.[4]

Designed and built by these men, Bittle Hall is a one-story Gothic Revival structure with a gable-end front. Hood molding tops a simple lancet window and doorway. Centered above these two units is a Gothic arched window (its arch having a radius larger than the two lancets below) with a circle and quatrefoil design; hood molding also tops this opening. A buttress with an octagonal finial is at each corner of the building.

A deep, pervasive concern with the past dominated nineteenth-century architecture. The Grecian forms dignified early-nineteenth-century building and gave young America architectural expression. By mid-century, however, new needs and attitudes prevailed. Many Americans felt that classical architecture no longer expressed their aspirations. The styles of the Middle Ages, on the other hand, accommodated romantic and idealistic yearnings by reminding people of the eternal qualities of Christianity. The Middle Ages were seen as a Christian religious era—as opposed to the paganism of ancient times. Americans, emulating the English, evoked the Middle Ages by using Gothic forms, and from the English revivals of medieval liturgical practices, they quickly gained a feeling that architecture should have a Christian moral purpose. The Greek Revival had a nationalistic didactic purpose, but the Gothic Revival with its aura of religious sanctity swept the country, so that by the end of the Civil War it was a dominant style. The country moved quickly from a few Gothic details on older structures to the building of entire churches and public buildings that attempted to recreate the Middle Ages. The early Gothic Revival did not reach its peak in southwest Virginia until the late nineteenth century. Bittle Hall at Roanoke College serves as an excellent example of religion-evoked Gothic architecture.

True Gothic form underwent centuries of development in Europe. The Renaissance coined the term *Gothic* to decry the culture inherited from the tribes of northern Europe. The term denigrated the style that is recognized today by its distinctive use of the vertical pointed arch. Although an integral part of original construction methods in Europe, the arch functions only as applied decoration in many nineteenth-century American buildings. Pinnacles, battlements, window tracery, and other medieval forms are used in America, but they were usually employed as purely decorative elements rather than as structural members. Bittle Hall's decorations and vertical massing render an excellent example of the early Gothic Revival style, even if they are late in date. The simple sharp gable, pointed arch, accents of thin tracery, and moldings of this style—as seen in this building—often give an appearance of fragility to the medieval decorative forms.

99
Johnsville Meetinghouse
Route 785, Roanoke County: Catawba
c. 1871–72

Seemingly overlooked by the passage of time, this German-Baptist meet-inghouse, still in use today, has changed little since its construction. Con-sisting of only one large room on the first floor with a small basement room below, the meetinghouse has a stone foundation, weatherboards on the outside, and a standing-seam sheet-metal roof. Two doors on the en-trance side allow the men and women to enter and sit separately, accord-ing to congregational custom. On each side of the severe building are three double-hung windows. Inside, in keeping with austere Protestant-ism, there is no altar, only pews facing a long table at which the deacons and minister sit during service. (See fig. 100.) Stained a dark red, the pews retain wavy marks from the hand planes that smoothed them. Two wood stoves provide the only heat. Wires strung from the ceiling on each side of the aisles serve to hold men's wide-brimmed hats. The unchanged interior provides an unusual architectural experience—"naturally-finished, uncluttered spaces are so rare in our culture."[1]

The building was erected in 1871–72 on a hill that once belonged to a Griffith John. In 1883, Griffith John's son, John John, acquired his father's land and deeded the three-fourths of an acre with the church on it to the German-Baptist congregation. Because the land was originally donated by the John family, the church is often called the Johnsville Meetinghouse. According to the minister of the church in 1978, the carpenter of the building may have been Nevon Wright, who had the help of the entire congregation.

In 1978, the congregation consisted of seventeen members,[2] who met at the church on the fourth Sunday of each month for a service and on the first weekend in October for a special Holy Communion service. For this latter service, the basement room serves as kitchen. Three Sundays a month the congregation worships at other area meetinghouses in shared services.

Churches mirror the beliefs of their congregations. For instance, the rural church created fundamentalist order in architecture, as well as in doctrine. The Johnsville Meetinghouse congregation keeps a simple, unadorned, white-painted building, impressive for its sparse purity; the simplicity and tranquility of the building creates its own spirituality.

100

**Johnsville Meetinghouse
(interior)
Route 785, Roanoke County
Catawba
c. 1871–72**

Virtually unchanged since it was built with simple, handcrafted materials, the interior of the Johnsville Meetinghouse has a sparse, unpretentious, yet religious quality all its own.

101
Nineteenth-Century Storefronts
17, 15, and 13 Campbell Avenue S.W., Roanoke City
c. 1890, c. 1890, 1889

Many nineteenth-century facades of commercial buildings that survived twentieth-century alterations to their first stories give character to Roanoke's older downtown streets. Three buildings on Campbell Avenue portray the diversity nineteenth-century businessmen chose for their establishments.

Arched windows with rich decoration in between give a vague Renaissance Revival look to the center building, built about 1890. The larger radius on the arch at the left of the center building adds a note of irregularity to the composition, but the use of arches as the main decorative pattern typifies this Renaissance style.

The Asberry Building (left), built about 1890 by A. S. Asberry, exemplifies the High-Victorian Italianate style. A distinctive pediment, strong moldings, and various ornamental, highly stylized shapes are features inspired by the freedom and eclecticism often associated with the Victorian period. The third store (right), dated 1889, has more of an Italian palazzo quality than the Asberry Building, but is similar to the center building in the Renaissance Revival details, the running scroll frieze, and the arcade of Corinthian columns. The building also carries an elaborate cornice with the date on it. This cornice, and many of the cornices on Roanoke's commercial buildings, probably came from companies such as the Roanoke Roofing and Metal Cornice Company, which was listed under "Cornice Companies" in the 1893–94 City Directory.[1]

After the arrival of the railroads, retail stores formed an important part of Roanoke's development. Enterprises prospered, and often a highly specialized establishment wanted prestige architecture for its storefront. Most of the nineteenth-century stores stood three stories high and were subdivided for offices and storage. The first commercial buildings were constructed with masonry supports, as in the Asberry Building, where a heavy appearance contrasts with the more delicate, classically derived forms next to it. Sheet metal, nailed on wooden framing, created the decoration. The rows of large windows with plate glass were also typical of the commercial style, as merchants in small cities tried to show off their new wealth as impressively as possible.

102
**Nineteenth-Century
Storefronts
116 and 114 Main Street
Salem
c. 1890**

A combination of Italianate, Roman, and Queen Anne forms was used on storefronts in the late nineteenth century. Although often the first and second stories of many such buildings were later renovated, the decorative upper stories were ignored until mid-twentieth-century interest in preservation called them to general attention.

103
Right-Angle House
413 High Street, Salem
c. 1870

Easily identifiable by its right-angle plan, the house in figure 103 is one of many variations of that plan throughout the valley. Despite additions to the original form, as well as a new door surround, the house retains a basic right-angle plan. The front door opens into a hall in the two-story wing next to the gable. According to records at the courthouse, J. R. C. Brown, Jr., owned the property until 1899.[1] The house was probably built soon after the Civil War.

New building forms sprang up everywhere after the Civil War. Several house types that were similar in plan came to the Roanoke area in the late nineteenth century. The right-angle house may be a T, an L, or a cross-plan, but it usually looks the same when viewed from the front. Generally, houses in this form have one gable roof perpendicular to the street and another gable roof parallel to it. Many later examples have semioctagonal bays, towers, and a wide variety of decoration. The right-angle form continued to be built and decorated in a variety of styles from the Gothic Revival to the early Queen Anne. In the northeastern United States the main door is often in the gable end; in the Midwest the door is usually in the wing. When the wing became two stories high in the late nineteenth century, the two-story L, T, or cross-plan house became common throughout the United States. Numerous examples of all three plans for the right-angle house may be seen in the Roanoke area.

104
Right-Angle House
728 Virginia Avenue, Salem
c. 1885
With a tower at the junction of its right angle, bay windows, and a cutout-design porch, this house belies its simple plan. As with the I house, the right-angle form showed a variety of elaborations during Salem's boom days.

105
Right-Angle House
518 Church Avenue S.W.
Roanoke City
c. 1880
Distinguished by its unusually fine state of preservation, this house in right-angle form has Italianate arched windows. Its porch decoration might well be described as whimsical. The fish-scale decoration on the roof and the variety of massed forms of the eaves indicate Queen Anne influence.

106

Right-Angle House
324 Fairview Avenue, Salem
c. 1885

Late-nineteenth-century decoration graces a right-angle form house. The curved brackets above the windows are an unusual and distinctive variation that lend style to the otherwise simple form. The spindles on the porch are in the Eastlake manner.

107

Right-Angle House
3911 Lee Highway S.W.
Roanoke City
c. 1870

The right-angle house was a form often built in this area after the Civil War. Like the I-form house, it received a variety of decorative treatments. Here overhanging bracketed eaves, a hooded window, and an arcaded porch all indicate the Italianate style.

108
Second Empire–Style House (Evans House)
213 Broad Street, Salem
1883
National Register 1972

Built in the Second Empire, or mansard, style, the Evans House has three bays across the front and two bays on each side. Two mansard sections meet at right angles to form the house's L shape. The main facade is symmetrically divided by a central mass that rises to a tower topped by an elongated square dome with finial. The design reflects the central plan of the interior. John M. Evans began building his residence in 1882

("$1,800 added for building unfinished"[1]), and it was completed the following year, when the value of the house was assessed at $4,300.[2] Family tradition relates that the house was a wedding present for Evans's French wife, who wanted her home to be in the French manner.

The style takes its name from the French Second Empire of Napoleon III (1852–70). Its main feature is a revival of the mansard roof combined with various Neo-Renaissance motifs. The steep sides of a mansard roof allow more headroom and light into the top story. A border often runs along the top of the slopes of the roof, and dormer windows are universally used. These windows are usually circular, as on the Evans House.

The Second Empire style became fashionable in America at a time when French ideas were enjoying popularity. It has also been called the General Grant style because it was in vogue during Grant's presidency (1869–77), but that name does not reflect its European origin. The style prevailed throughout the 1880s, although American architects often took liberties with it by combining other decorative motifs with the basic Second Empire style. Because this style has been used in modern cartoons, the architecture is often called Charles Addams style.

The mansard style was easily adapted to both public and domestic architecture. The Evans House is a distinctive small variation on that style and would stand out in any American community. Usually, however, a Second Empire–style house would be larger than the Evans House, with the mansard forming a third, attic story.

Neo-Renaissance motifs can be seen in details such as the brackets under the cornices, the shape of the pediments over the windows, and the columns and pilasters on the front porch. The house's rich use of moldings, brackets, and various forms of gingerbread is also typical of the Neo-Renaissance. An unusual feature of the exterior is that all the trim—the cornices, brackets, eaves, pendants, scrolls, dormer frames, window hoods, rakings, and ornamental carvings—is carved wood that has been sheathed in metal. The decoration is literally bolted on! The unknown architect of the John M. Evans House designed a building that conveyed the Second Empire style with nineteenth-century liveliness. Intricately carved scrolls, cornices, and brackets, as well as Neo-Renaissance symmetry, add formality to its eclectic style; in an era when picturesque asymmetry and profuse use of decoration were popular, this house shows remarkable restraint. Cast-iron windowsills and rectangular plates under the bay windows add decorative accents to the exterior. On the front porch and on the interior doors of the first floor, the imported solid-brass hardware beautifully complements the rich colors of the wood, and all these intricate fixtures typify the richness of the entire house.

118

109
Evans House (detail)
213 Broad Street, Salem
1883

The beautiful craftsmanship on the exterior of this house was continued in the interior. The newel post suggests the Gothic style with cluster columns, Gothic arches, and a high finial.

110
Second Empire–Style Building
Academy Street School
113 Academy Street, Salem
1890
National Register 1980

Unfortunately, this school lost its Second Empire mansard tower. Its floor plan is unusual; inside on both floors, classrooms open to an octagonal central hall.

111
Second Empire–Style House
1405 Patterson Avenue S.W.
Roanoke City
c. 1890

The distinctive mansard roof and tower are belied by the later wraparound porch. Houses in the Second Empire style are usually symmetrical—as here. Paint, storm windows, and other additions have almost obscured the formal grandeur of this stylish residence.

112
Queen Anne–Style House
414 Walnut Avenue S.W., Roanoke City
1909

Basically a cube form, this large house built in 1909 has innumerable projections. Dominant features include the balustraded porch, the Ionic columns, the dentil moldings on the entablature, and a turret over a balcony, as well as a large gable with a Palladian window in it. All of these informally massed large details typify the Queen Anne style. Classical details, such as the pediment over the entrance, the Ionic columns around the porch, and the Palladian window, reflect the coming of the Colonial Revival style. The use of different textures fascinated builders of the Queen Anne style. Weatherboard not only accentuates the horizontal effect but gives richness to the surface. Fish-scale designs in the roof tile and in the prominent gable contrast with the horizontal weatherboarding. Windows also add to the overall effect; on the first floor are large plate-glass panes with panels of diamond-shaped stained glass above. Bay windows on the second floor, below the gable, give more depth to the exterior. Window

120

placement, the deep porch, and the open turret all work together to create effects of mass and space that are so strategic to the Queen Anne style.

In the late nineteenth and early twentieth centuries, the style rose to popularity. The name of the style does not imply a relationship to the architecture styles prevalent during the rule of Queen Anne in England (1702–14). Queen Anne style is actually an amalgamation—highly eclectic, as are other late-nineteenth-century architectural movements. It began as a mixture of English country-house styles that had Jacobean gables, Tudor massing, fake half-timbering, and English baroque details during the 1870s. The style first came to notice in America at the Philadelphia Centennial Exposition of 1876, where the British government pavilion, built in the Queen Anne manner, was admired. Used innovatively in America, this informal, flexible style was one of the first breakaways from Victorian Revivalism. The Queen Anne style no longer conformed to accepted canons of taste.

Builders and advocates of the Queen Anne style stressed the importance of its individuality. They felt that the various types of decoration and the random massing of the house added a personal touch. Often the search for architectural inspiration led Queen Anne–style builders back to American Colonial architecture. Eighteenth-century forms fused with Queen Anne–style forms. The Palladian window on Walnut Avenue is an example. The Queen Anne style created an architecture that many Americans felt was honest. Roanoke accepted this style, and there are many examples of it in older sections of Roanoke City and Salem dating from the boom period between the coming of the railroad and World War I.

113
Queen Anne–Style House
5415 Plantation Road, Roanoke
County
c. 1882

Located away from Plantation Road, so that it is difficult to see except in winter, this Queen Anne–style house is made of brick with white millwork trim. Bay windows, balconies, and bargeboards in the Eastlake manner produce irregularity and informality typical of the late nineteenth century. Two full stories and an attic give the house high, narrow proportions and show a desire for picturesque effects. Note the pointed-arch windows of the earlier Gothic style.

114

Queen Anne–Style House
415 Pennsylvania Avenue
Salem
1887

Eastlake-style decoration on Queen Anne houses always looks like the turnings and cutout work seen on furniture of the period. Here, the large masses of a Queen Anne house have been ornamented with a variety of millwork in the Eastlake fashion. The decoration was created by the use of chisels, gouges, and lathes, but rarely with saws. Many of the designs were borrowed from furniture with knobs and decorative motifs consisting of circular perforation. Curved brackets appear everywhere. Posts often look like table legs. Spindles forming friezes, finials, and drop pendants proliferated according to the wealth of the owner.

As with many style names, the term Eastlake style is imprecise. Charles L. Eastlake (1836–1906) was an English architect and writer whose books served as models for furniture makers. Eastlake endeavored to guide his readers in finding picturesque qualities that would not mean the sacrifice of comfort and convenience. The furniture style named for Eastlake precipitated the architectural style. America's version of Eastlake, in architecture and in furniture, frequently provided the stimulus for machine-made decoration. As industry grew in the Roanoke Valley with the arrival of the railroads, the technological advances of the nineteenth century were immediately utilized in architecture. The gingerbread on this house demonstrates the kind of architectural embellishments made possible by machines. Worked with steam power or waterpower, the new tools cut out scrolls and turned decoration. Probably other examples of the style (rather than Eastlake's books) inspired the Eastlake decoration on this particular house.

115
Queen Anne–Style House
125 Elm Avenue S.W.
Roanoke City
c. 1890

The delicate spindles and turnings on the front of this house are in the Eastlake manner, which was often applied on the surface of late-nineteenth-century Queen Anne houses. The alternating reversed positions of the spindles around the porch adds a note of whimsy typical of the Eastlake style.

116
Queen Anne–Style House
1010 First Street S.W.
Roanoke City
c. 1890

Always varied and richly decorated with a great variety of shapes, textures, and materials, the Queen Anne style was the fashionable, informal style of the late nineteenth century. Towers and turrets are typical, as are projections and verandas surrounding the building.

117
Queen Anne–Style House
(detail)
1010 First Street S.W.
Roanoke City
c. 1890

Queen Anne–style buildings combine a variety of flat textured surfaces on various projecting dormers, towers, and turrets. Fish-scale patterns, in both shingles and roof slates, were used consistently to create picturesque effects.

118
Queen Anne–Style House
1501 Patterson Avenue S.W.
Roanoke City
1890–91

The large square house, built for Col. Augustus Pope in 1890–91, is capped by an octagonal turret and surrounded by a wide veranda. Rock-faced masonry covers the exterior. This rough stone covering is unusual in Roanoke. Stone courses separating the stories, the polygon turret, heavy chimney, and dormers relate in shape to the Queen Anne style.

119
Queen Anne–Style Railroad Station
1031 College Avenue, Salem
1891

Designed in 1890 by Philadelphia architect George T. Pearson, Salem's Queen Anne–style railroad station represents the new prosperity of that city in the late nineteenth century. In less than fifteen months, between October 1889 and January 1891, the population of Salem nearly doubled. For that time the up-to-date style of this station must have been a fitting entry to the booming little city. Note the wide overhanging hip roof with decorative ridge flashing and hip knob, as well as the imitation half-timber central portion can be seen in this 1917 picture.

120
**Queen Anne–Style Railroad
Station
1031 College Avenue, Salem
1891**

A 1953 drawing done for a proposed consolidation of freight and passenger facilities at Salem shows the Queen Anne building and the station platform connected by a stairway. This station is an unusual example of a Queen Anne–style building used for commercial purposes.

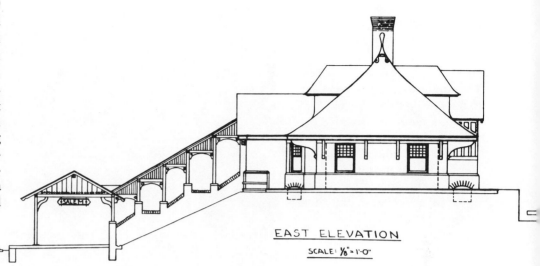

EAST ELEVATION

SCALE: ⅛" = 1'-0"

121
**Queen Anne–Style House
424 High Street, Salem
c. 1890**

Millwork decoration in a variety of fanciful forms is typical of the Queen Anne style. Asymmetrical placement of the decoration also adds to the informal air so desired by home builders of this period.

125

122

Queen Anne–Style House
836 Campbell Avenue S.W.
Roanoke City
c. 1890

The late Queen Anne style tends to be more rigid and geometric, with elements carefully disposed on the surface. The rounded exuberance of the earlier Queen Anne gives way to squared-off shapes. The interest in texture remains, but it is more restrained.

123

Queen Anne–Style House
1144 Second Street S.W.
Roanoke City
c. 1900

In the late phases of the Queen Anne style there is not as much variety in texture, but the informal massing is retained. Here historical references have been dropped in favor of picturesque textures and groupings of roof forms. Later in the twentieth century the massing seen here is typically ornamented with Old English details.

124
Administration Building (formerly called Charles L. Cocke Memorial)
Hollins College
Route 11, Roanoke County: Hollins
1908
National Register 1974

Charles L. Cocke (1820–1901), founder of Hollins College, devoted his life to the intellectual development of young women. To honor him, the Charles L. Cocke Memorial Library was built in 1908 from the designs of the Lynchburg, Virginia, architectural firm of Frye and Chesterman.[1] The last building constructed on the quadrangle, it closed off the south side. Dominating the campus today, it is proportionally larger than the other buildings. The imposing edifice compares with Stanford White's Cabell Hall (1898–1902)—which closed off the south end of Thomas Jefferson's Lawn at the University of Virginia.

The Charles L. Cocke Library was converted into administration offices in 1955, but the overscaled structure continues to dominate the campus with its large Ionic portico of six columns resting on a stepped platform, all in Neoclassical style. Featuring large, simple effects with less decoration than Beaux-Arts classicism, the Neoclassical style is often called the Second Greek Revival, the American Renaissance, or the Academic Reaction. Museums and civic buildings often use this important American style.

127

125
Roanoke City Municipal Building
210 Campbell Avenue S.W. Roanoke City
1915

Built to house the municipal offices, this Neoclassical Revival style building has three large projecting bays facing Campbell Avenue. The two end bays accommodate paired Ionic columns, while the center bay has four Ionic columns in antis (see fig. 126). The building has a large entablature with a terra-cotta frieze; decorated moldings and an inscription hang over the center bay. Both the columns and the brick pilasters are two stories high, visually uniting the entire building. The whole structure sits on a base in the Roman manner. Made of brick and stone, the building was an imposing addition to a growing city.

As early as 1907, Roanoke City considered appropriating a $100,000 bond issue for a suitable municipal building. The plans of the local architectural firm of Frye and Chesterman, who were first listed as Roanoke architects in 1913,[1] were accepted on July 12, 1913, and on September 15, 1914, the city accepted the lowest bid of $218,900 for construction, which came from the King Lumber Company of Charlottesville, Virginia. The same firm had built the County Courthouse in 1909, but unfortunately it went bankrupt before the completion of the municipal building.

The structure was finished, however, because of the surety on the bond of the contractor.

Neoclassical Revival–style buildings tend to exhibit strength and energy in contrast to the quiet, simple Greek Revival style. Neoclassical Revival forms stand forth boldly; projections from the mass form an important part of the composition. Large entablatures play off against massive shapes. There are often monumental flights of stairs (as in the Municipal Building) and an elaborate approach to symmetry, usually a five-part composition with a central mass dominating. The use of advancing and receding planes—violating classical canons—is also common. A pictorial approach to composition marks buildings in this manner as important early-twentieth-century architectural scenery for many cities.

126
Roanoke City Municipal
Building (detail)
210 Campbell Avenue S.W.
Roanoke City
1915
Over a monumental staircase, large-scale classical ornament in profusion signifies the solidity and dignity of the city of Roanoke in the early twentieth century.

127
Roanoke City Municipal
Building (modern addition)
215 Church Avenue S.W.
Roanoke City
1971
Neoclassical Revival massing and forms have been repeated in a pared-down manner for this addition, designed by Hayes, Seay, Mattern and Mattern, to the earlier Municipal Building. Various textures were substituted for the Neoclassical decoration on the earlier Municipal Building.

128

**House Decorated in
Neoclassical Revival Style
223 Broad Street, Salem
c. 1867, 1905**

In 1905 a new facade, featuring double-story Corinthian columns, a decorated entablature, and a wide veranda supported by Ionic columns, was added to the original cube-form house. The Italianate house was overwhelmed by this classical style decoration. According to family legend, a son of the original owner visited Chicago—undoubtedly to see the World's Columbian Exposition of 1893—and brought home pictures and drawings that persuaded his father to remodel the simple facade in Neoclassical style.

129

**House Decorated in
Neoclassical Revival Style
(detail)
223 Broad Street, Salem
c. 1867, 1905**

After the 1905 renovation of the earlier Italianate-style house (fig. 128), splendid Roman Corinthian columns, supporting a massive entablature, overpowered the Italianate windows.

130

130
Bank and Office Building
210 Jefferson Street S.W.
Roanoke City
1909

Classical forms were used on the ground floor to create an impressive banking atmosphere. Six stories of office space above the ground floor culminate in brackets and an overscaled balustrade. The combination of yellow brick and cut stone is often found on buildings in the Roanoke Valley.

131
The First National Exchange
Bank Building
201 Jefferson Street S.W.
Roanoke City
c. 1935

Strong use of classical motifs and variations on Roman forms are seen in this unusual composition. Dominated by large Ionic columns below a heavy entablature, the bank's stability and financial security were well conveyed by the massive classical design of Wyatt and Nolting of Baltimore, as seen in this 1930 photograph.

132
Renaissance Revival–Style House
2855 Jefferson Street S.E., Roanoke City
1929

Although the style is common in large cities, the Italian-Renaissance Revival occurs infrequently in Roanoke. Arched loggia, simple stucco walls, and a low roof with cornice emphasis gives a Renaissance mode to this Jefferson Street residence. Renaissance detailing, in stucco rather than marble, creates a picturesque quality. More varied than the Georgian (see the following section) in its source borrowings, the style never really became popular in America.

Henry J. Boynton, architect of the Roanoke firm of Smithey and Tardy, designed this 1929 home for Charles Wilson. According to recent owners, the Wilsons had the parent plans drawn in Italy to reproduce a villa they admired. The use of marble and tile on the inside (as here; see fig. 133) is a common trait of Renaissance Revival. Oral history relates that these materials were sent from Italy, as were the conspicuous balusters of the front terraces. Other materials came from the Roanoke Marble and Granite Company, which Mr. Wilson owned.[1] The house is an excellent example of the Renaissance Revival style seen in many major cities and at northeastern resorts.

133
Renaissance Revival–Style
House (detail)
2855 Jefferson Street S.E.
Roanoke City
1929
Inside details in the Renaissance Revival manner feature marble columns and wrought-iron decorations that are typical of the extravagance of that era. The Corinthian columns on the interior repeat those seen on the exterior.

134
Firehouse no. 1
13 Church Avenue S.E., Roanoke City, 1907–8
National Register 1972

From the days of horse-drawn fire equipment to motorized hook-and-ladder trucks, a working fire department has been housed in this building for most of the twentieth century. Built in 1907–8, it was designed by Roanoke architect H. H. Huggins.[1] The brick facade and the well-preserved interior and appointments make the building one of Roanoke's most important landmarks. Foundation stones of rough-hewn limestone support brick walls that are rusticated on the first story, with arches and pilasters above. A bell tower, or cupola, rises from a low-sloped roof. The roof is hidden on the facade by a brick parapet and on the sides by step forms. The facade has two large double doors that still retain the original hardware. A small door in the center serves as a pedestrian entrance. The second-floor facade windows are set in arched recesses framed by Corinthian pilasters and stone keystones.

Inside the firehouse, many of the original fittings remain. These furnishings attracted a newspaper reporter to write an article describing the building and calling it to the public's attention. " . . . What's impressive about it is that nothing in it looks like it's been touched or moved in years. It's not a replica of what a room looked like in the past, but the real thing."[2] Ceilings 16½ feet tall and ridged floors that once gave horses traction create a back-in-time mood. An embossed tin ceiling, painted silver, has many of the early light fixtures still hanging (fig. 135). The original brass poles descend through openings in the tin ceiling. The second floor houses eight rooms with unfinished maple floors and tin ceilings (fig. 136). On the same floor, one hayloft serves for storage, another has been converted to a kitchen. In the 1930s pine wainscotting on the walls of the chief's office was painted brownish-yellow and beautifully comb-grained.

The facade of the firehouse is a diverse mixture of styles often termed Colonial Revival or Georgian Revival. Much of the decoration, however, was derived from the English style of Sir Christopher Wren (1632–1723), humorously referred to as "Wrennaissance." Roanoke's Firehouse no. 1 and the Georgian style of Independence Hall in Philadelphia share some common features.[3] The Wren style set the pattern for the style called Georgian, a term derived from the reigns of the four Georges: George I, 1714–27; George II, 1727–60; George III, 1760–1820; George IV, 1820–30. Popularly, the term *Colonial* has been used for any style that looks back to America's eighteenth-century, English-derived architectural heritage. Historians of architecture call the adaptations Georgian Revival, but many aspects of the style are drawn from the American Federal Period. The work of Robert Adam, who practiced architecture in England between 1760 and 1780, inspired the Adamesque style, called Federal in America. The American Georgian (dominant here until the time of the American Revolution) and the Adamesque styles together comprise the Georgian Revival, or (as it is more commonly called) the Colonial. The word *Colonial* has been used excessively and is full of so many patriotic, historic overtones that it is as impossible to define as the word *Gothic*.[4] Each age develops its own words for expressing cultural ideas. *Colonial* may have originally reflected an ideal of excellence, but now the word simply gives approbation. In real estate jargon, *Colonial* refers to houses having eighteenth-century decoration.

Colonial-style structures—whether residences, churches, or public buildings—are generally rectangular in shape with minimal projections; they often have strictly symmetrical facades. Roof forms are hipped, double pitched, or gambrel, and cornices are often treated with classical dentil moldings. Railings, balustrades, and other Georgian and Adam-esque forms are used randomly, but in symmetrical arrangements. Pediments—plain or in swan's neck form—crown entrances. Doorways often have fanlights, and windows have double-hung sashes with small panes. The Palladian window often becomes a focal point. Churches have square towers with complex superstructures that get smaller and more octagonal before ending in spires. Even when twentieth century buildings, such as civic monuments, are too large to imitate prototypes, these effects are created by taking Colonial units and multiplying them. In the early twentieth century, the problem was (and still remains) how to adapt the old designs to modern needs. Even though the revival may seem incongruous in the twentieth century, the Colonial style still speaks forcefully to a majority of Americans—perhaps because the country has romanticized the eighteenth century just as the eighteenth century romanticized the Middle Ages. If there is an architectural style that is generally accepted all over America, it is the Colonial style.

The 1876 Centennial Exhibition in Philadelphia brought Colonial Revival buildings to public attention. Many viewers perceived the buildings as representing a return to restraint and simplicity after the casual picturesque quality of many mid-century revivals of other styles.[5] From the 1870s until well into the twentieth century, architects gained more knowledge of actual eighteenth-century American buildings by drawing, measuring, and photographing old buildings to create source material. During World War I—a period in which America seemed to lack confidence in the quality of its own contemporary work—the nation admired older American products and decried European styles in favor of Colonial revivals. In the United States from 1915 to 1940 the Weyerhaeuser Lumber Company published the famous *White Pine* architectural monographs, which advocated wooden Colonial Revival architecture—furthering both the style's popularity and profits for the lumber business.

Since World War I, many architects may have had only vague ideas concerning the true history and development of architecture, but they have used early American forms indiscriminately to signify hospitality, cheerfulness, and the good old days. Great mansions as well as modest cottages were built in the Georgian Revival manner, taking advantage of the low costs of material and labor to create simple shapes and a large floor space. Late-nineteenth- and early-twentieth-century architects admired the fine quality of eighteenth-century craftsmanship in contrast to the machine work that surrounded them. According to William B. Rhoads, on the other hand, as early as 1882 a perceptive architect saw that modern builders "would not tolerate the oversize beams, irregular boards, leaking roofs, irregular and imperfectly burned bricks, primitive plumbing, small closets, tiny windows, and crooked stairs commonly found in the Colonial House."[6]

From the 1890s through today, the popularity of Colonial domestic architecture and the Spanish and English revivals have been integrally related to the development of the suburbs—those new belts of residential areas between the inner city and the country. In the 1920s and 1930s, lot sizes became larger. Before 1890 and the suburban development, the first floor of most American homes rose three or four feet above the ground. The revival houses sit lower on the ground and give direct access to a terrace. Porches are generally small, or at right angles to the building, rather than being wrapped around as on the Victorian and Queen Anne houses. A continuing problem with the revival house has been how to provide it with a veranda while retaining its Colonial, Spanish, or Old English appearance. Open rooms, long one-story designs, and outdoor living areas characterize the informal plans of suburban houses. New child-parent relationships, servant shortages, central heat, and gas and electric appliances have all affected the pattern of suburban development.

The Colonial Revival began in the Queen Anne–style period, when textured shingles began to give way to clapboards, brick and millwork trim that copied eighteenth-century style. Symmetry, rather than picturesque effect, became important. The Queen Anne roof, previously of various forms, became hipped or gabled in the Georgian manner. Early Colonial Revival forms appear broad and bulky; their decoration rarely harmonized with their large roofs. The big porches of the Queen Anne were often retained, and architects also continued to use the corner tower. After 1900, however, there was a greater focus on symmetry and refinement. Later decoration was carefully integrated by correct proportions and detail derived from actual prototypes. By 1910 the Colonial Revival might be called Neo-Georgian, and by 1920 the Colonial style embodied a serious and learned architecture to be used on houses, churches, and civic buildings in a pedantic manner. Directly imitating massing, proportions, materials, and even details of an individual older style, a Colonial Revival building clearly reflected its source, as was not always the case in the

1890s. This exact borrowing holds true also for the Spanish and Old English styles. However, archeological correctness in Colonial Revival architecture was not brought to fruition until the 1940s, after the development of Colonial Williamsburg.

In the 1920s and 1930s the Colonial style swept this country, as houses went up at an ever faster rate in newly developing suburbs.[7] Sinclair Lewis caught the spirit of the trend particularly well in 1922: "Babbitt's green and white Colonial was one of three in that block . . . it was all . . . competent and glossy. . . . It had the best of taste."[8] The Colonial, with a second story tucked up under a picturesque roof, was a favorite form of plan-book makers and speculative builders. Languishing in the dreary plains of the Middle West, Carol Kennicott, the frustrated heroine of Sinclair Lewis's *Main Street*, longed for a Georgian city hall, a Georgian town, and her own Georgian home as she perused magazines about interior decoration and city planning.[9] George F. Babbitt and Carol Kennicott represented American enthusiasm for replicas, reconstructed historical atmosphere, and pretentious architecture. The appeal of Colonial Revival buildings continues through our own time. Nostalgia for the past—some would say for the architecture of an aristocracy, along with its class distinctions[10]—has undoubtedly stimulated pride in America's first architecture. The Colonial Revival prevails.

135
Firehouse no. 1 (detail)
13 Church Avenue S.E.
Roanoke City
1907–8
The elaborate embossed tin ceiling above the first floor of the firehouse is painted silver and has some of the original flowerlike light fixtures still in place.

Firehouse no. 1 (detail)
13 East Church Avenue S.E.
Roanoke City
1907–8

Part of the second floor of the firehouse is still used as a sleeping room for the firemen. Original unfinished maple floors, pine woodwork now painted brownish-yellow and comb grained, and built-in wooden lockers are still intact. Even the "Firehouse" Windsor chairs remain.

---

137 Mountain View (City of Roanoke Recreation Center)
726 Thirteenth Street S.W.
Roanoke City
1908
National Register 1981

On a four-acre plot, this forty-two room mansion was designed by Roanoke architect H. H. Huggins for Junius Blair Fishburn, banker and principal owner of Roanoke's daily newspapers for almost thirty-five years. The house was built of Washington pressed brick with a green tile roof. A stable, a garage, a greenhouse, and servants' quarters were on the property. American Colonial Revival style was mixed with English Georgian features for maximum impressiveness.

**Mountain View (City of
Roanoke Recreation Center)
(detail)
726 Thirteenth Street S.W.
Roanoke City
1908**

The impressive center stair hall
of Mountain View imitates the
English heritage of Georgian architecture. Well-preserved light
fixtures are an unusual survival.
The front hall of Mountain View
is one of the finest domestic interiors in this area.

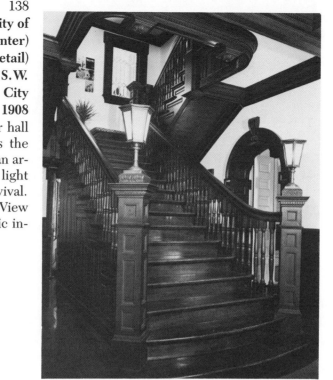

**Mountain View (City of
Roanoke Recreation Center)
(detail)
726 Thirteenth Street S.W.
Roanoke City
1908**

A curved solarium surrounds
the dining room of Mountain
View—offering a view of plants
and flowers, with gardens beyond, in the south light. An
original light fixture, leaded-glass
windows, marble encased radia-
tors, and tile floor with drain
create an impressive greenhouse setting seen through the
dining room windows of this Colonial Revival style home.

Colonial Revival–Style House
317 Washington Avenue S.W.
Roanoke City
c. 1910

The symmetry introduced by the Colonial Revival in the early twentieth century is well illustrated here. While each eighteenth-century feature is correct in itself, the massing and recombination of features shows an inventiveness and freedom that lasts in the Colonial Revival until the 1940s.

Colonial Revival–Style House
441 Highland Avenue S.W.
Roanoke City
c. 1910

The transition from the Queen Anne style to the Colonial Revival style is seen in this circa 1910 photograph. Queen Anne informality, irregularity, and asymmetry has given way to formal Doric columns; regular, if overscaled, dentil moldings and details; and rigidly symmetrical placement of every feature. The massiveness admired in the late nineteenth and early twentieth centuries is retained despite the change of style. The wraparound porch of the Victorian era is all that remains of the informality of the nineteenth century. Colonial Revival pretentiousness was to dominate a great deal of building in Roanoke in the early twentieth century.

142
Colonial Revival–Style House
903 Jefferson Street S.W.
Roanoke City
c. 1910

High-style Colonial Revival buildings took on many features from American and English Georgian architecture. Diverse architectural embellishments of the eighteenth century are freely used. Most Colonial Revival buildings are larger, thanks to modern technology, than eighteenth-century Georgian structures.

143
Roanoke County Courthouse
305 East Main Street, Salem
1909

H. H. Huggins was the architect and King Lumber Company of Charlottesville the builder of a new courthouse to replace one that burned in 1907. By 1909, when this building was finished (photograph taken about 1920), it represented a style that may be described as Classical, even though it also contained Colonial, Roman, and Beaux-Arts style elements!

144

Roanoke County Courthouse
(detail)
305 East Main Street, Salem
1909

The cupola on the Roanoke County Courthouse is in an amalgamation of styles—Colonial Revival and Renaissance Revival. A soaring American eagle caps the cupola.

145

Colonial Revival–Style House
1857 Grandin Road S.W.
Roanoke City
1916

The Colonial Revival style often used American Federal–style decorative motifs. While the details were technically derived from post-revolutionary American architecture, they conveyed eighteenth-century feeling. The broad, squat proportions of the Georgian style here were embellished with light, delicate Adamesque details.

146
City Market
32 Campbell Avenue S.E.
Roanoke City
1922

Completed in 1922 to replace an earlier market building, this structure was designed by E. G. Frye, Roanoke architect, in the Colonial Revival style. The structure has a central pedimented block with flanking wings; the whole forms an H shape. Around the outside, over the first story, is a metal canopy. The interior of the first floor houses a meat market, and on the second floor there is a large auditorium. The style, with its American associative qualities, has always been popular in the Roanoke Valley.

147
City Market (detail)
32 Campbell Avenue S.E.
Roanoke City
1922

A farmers' curb market, with the City Market building as background, is a bustling center of activity in Roanoke City.

**148
United States Post Office
(doorway detail)
103 East Main Street, Salem
1923**

American Colonial Revival details are often overscaled. Here, what appears to be a Georgian handbook-derived doorcase is representative of the 1920s interest in correctness of detail, though reproduced on a larger scale.

U·S·POST·OFFICE·

103 EAST MAIN ST.
SALEM VA. 24153

Colonial Revival–Style House
101 Twenty-seventh Street
S.W., Roanoke City
1925

Attempting to capture eighteenth-century America and
English Georgian style, Roanoke architect Robert M. Allen
designed this large-scale house
in the Colonial Revival style.
Composite columns—a combination of the Corinthian and
Ionic orders used by the Romans—support an elaborately
carved pediment that recalls
English Chippendale design.
The swan's neck pediment is a
typical Georgian feature seen in
both England and America in
the eighteenth century.

150
Colonial Revival–Style House
(detail)
101 Twenty-seventh Street
S.W.
Roanoke City
c. 1910

The swan's neck pediment remains a favorite of American
builders working in the colonial
styles. Overscaled to suit this
large house, the ornate pediment caps the central doorway
in the Georgian manner.

151
Colonial Revival–Style House
2120 Carter Road S.W.
Roanoke City
c. 1925

A gambrel roof and a Federal-appearing doorway are semiaccurate historical features, but the arched porch, the thin columns, and one-story wings are creative reinterpretations. All are typical of the Colonial Revival prior to World War II. Houses such as this were very popular in the growing suburban areas.

152
Colonial Revival–Style Houses
Wiley Court
Locust Avenue, Salem
1936–37

Surrounding a "village green," eight identical colonial-style cottages create a little enclave with eighteenth-century atmosphere in Salem. A farsighted developer put a service road behind this semicircle of houses, leaving the open green for atmosphere.

153
Store
Oak Grove Plaza, Roanoke
County
c. 1970

The proportions and some of the decorations of Mount Vernon are used to evoke a colonial atmosphere. The Colonial Revival is still popular today.

154
St. Andrew's Roman Catholic Church
631 Jefferson Street N.E., Roanoke City
1902
National Register 1972

St. Andrew's Church in Roanoke is one of the most distinguished examples of High Victorian Gothic architecture in Virginia. Based loosely on French Gothic sources, the design follows that of French medieval churches: a cruciform plan with narthex, transept, and apse. The seven-sided apse contains the altar. Twin spires that tower over the city exemplify the best High Victorian Gothic tradition.[1]

The yellow brick exterior manifests the High Victorian love of color. Bands of dark stone set off this color and add further textural interest. Yellow brick, incidentally, was chosen because its hard finish would resist the dirt and grime of a railroad town. The foundation is made of rough stones topped by a water table of smooth stone. Fourteen steps lead up to the traditional three front doors. Above each door is a stained-glass transom. A stained-glass rose window highlights the center of the facade, and in a niche above this window stands a stone statue of St. Andrew holding the cross of his martyrdom. Over the center of the nave is a small crossing-tower. On the side walls are four lancet-shaped windows with wooden tracery. Even more elaborate tracery fills the end walls of the transepts. The seven-sided apse at the altar end of the building is the climax of the building.

The church's interior is even more elaborate than its exterior. Richly decorated and colorful with medieval forms freely adapted, the nave seats 800 worshipers on long pews. Gothic motifs in white marble cover the ornate altar in the apse. An elaborate system of ribbed vaults ending in ornately carved pendants supports the ceiling above the apse. (See fig. 155.) Bright stained glass windows depicting various religious scenes such as the Annunciation and the Last Supper add further atmosphere to the interior. One transept window pictures St. Patrick and the other transept window shows St. Andrew. The upper west wall displays the rose window with a medallion of St. Cecilia, patron saint of musicians, surrounded by angels and floral designs.

Painted and stenciled decoration on the walls of the interior (fig. 156) is unusual. Executed in the 1940s by artists unknown today, the work looks Victorian. Above a molding of simulated stone lies a band of gold leaf with red, blue, and green in a vine and rose motif. Flowers and crosses run along the edge of the nave wall windows. A vine pattern in red, blue, and gold adorns ribs of the vaulting. Polychromed statues of angels holding banners decorate colorful niches of the choir. Reds and blues cover the lower walls, and there is a deep blue background above with a field of stars that resembles the heavens. This decoration, along with the use of gold leaf on the pendants and column capitals, creates a rich effect in the large space. In 1975, the entire decor was beautifully restored by Walt O'Brien of the firm of Fred M. Botcher and Son in Elmira, New York.

The history of St. Andrew's Roman Catholic Church dates back to November 19, 1882, when Father John W. Lynch, a newly ordained priest, offered the first Mass to his Roman Catholic congregation in passenger coach no. 6 of the Shenandoah Valley Railroad. For twelve months the passenger car served as his church. When J. B. Austin, a land developer, offered Father Lynch any unclaimed site in his company's holdings, he chose two acres atop what is now St. Andrew's Hill. The first little church was erected on the hill's crest, and the congregation grew and prospered. Father Lynch then initiated plans for a larger church. William P. Ginther of Akron, Ohio, was hired as architect, and on December 2, 1900, ground-breaking ceremonies were held for a new structure. John J. Garry oversaw construction of the $100,000 building. On November 25, 1902, the new church was dedicated. A wooden belfry reportedly from the old church is displayed today on the grounds.

The heyday of the High Victorian Gothic style in the United States occurred in the 1870s. Ginther's design for St. Andrew's reflects a popular church style, which emphasizes weight and color effects. Use of contrasting colors and materials differentiates this late Gothic from the earlier Gothic Revival. The forms of High Victorian Gothic are resplendent with many small details, particularly on the towers and the roof lines. There is no gingerbread here; the structure is solid and enduring. Architecturally, St. Andrew's ranks as one of the largest and finest examples of High Victorian Gothic style in Virginia.

155
St. Andrew's Roman Catholic Church (detail)
631 Jefferson Street N.E.
Roanoke City
1902

Beneath soaring polychromed vaults, the white Italian marble altar of St. Andrew's Church forms the terminus of one of the most impressive religious spaces in the Roanoke Valley.

156
**St. Andrew's Roman Catholic
Church (detail)
631 Jefferson Street N.E.
Roanoke City
1902**
Ornate stencil work and gilding
on the vaulting of St. Andrew's
was beautifully restored in 1975.

157
First Presbyterian Church
2101 Jefferson Street S.W., Roanoke City
1929; addition, 1965

Leaving their old building in the congested downtown area, the First Presbyterian Church congregation built a new large stone church in 1929 in the fast-developing residential section of southwest Roanoke.[1] The complex included a chancel and a front entrance, with a high tower joining the main building to an office wing. An education building and a chapel connected to the original structure were completed in 1965. The architect of the first building was Louis Philippe Smithey of Roanoke, with Meyer and Mathieu of Brooklyn, New York, as consulting architects. J. Walker Caldwell of Roanoke designed the 1965 addition. The chancel, the tower, and the stained-glass window above the front doorway follow basic Gothic designs. Large blocks of Catawba stone have been rusticated to create a heavy medieval effect. A series of six massive buttresses support each side of the nave to form side aisles. To give an illusion of height, reinforcements on the tower corners diminish in size as they approach the top. The tower is not situated on the same axis as the nave—probably for visual effect.

Nineteenth- and twentieth-century American architecture borrowed from three separate periods of European Gothic sources. In Roanoke these three styles are explicit in Bittle Hall at Roanoke College (1879), St. Andrew's Roman Catholic Church (1902), and First Presbyterian Church (1929). Bittle Hall (fig. 98), in the Early Gothic Revival style, has light, delicate decoration with sharp-pointed arches and moldings; St. Andrew's Church (fig. 154), in the High Victorian Gothic style, uses loosely derived and eclectic Gothic sources and a great number of coloristic effects; while the Late Gothic Revival style of First Presbyterian draws upon English Perpendicular Gothic architecture. Small parish churches rather than great cathedrals characterized the Perpendicular Gothic style period in England from 1350 to the Reformation in 1534, and these simpler forms appealed to American architects in the period between the two world wars.

Stone and masonry lend a strong, substantial look to First Presbyterian Church, as do stone tracery and heavy detailing. High standards of craftsmanship and a consistent vertical emphasis mark both the original 1929 building and the 1965 addition. Built of the same Catawba stone, but at a right angle to the office complex, the 1965 addition forms another block in the composition. With its picturesque grouping of English-derived forms, First Presbyterian Church achieves a pleasing informality as well as dignity.

158
First Presbyterian Church
(detail, front door)
2101 Jefferson Street S.W.
Roanoke City
1929; addition 1965
Broad areas of masonry set off the stained glass in the tympanum, the stylized flowers in the archivolt, and the ornate hinges on the door. Medieval forms were reused in a new context in the Late Gothic Revival style—America's third Gothic revival.

159
Jefferson High School
550 Campbell Avenue S.W., Roanoke City
1924

Jefferson High School's proportions, detailing, and visual dominance bespeak the importance given to educational structures in the 1920s. Built of brick and stone, its distinctive facade faces Campbell Avenue. At the top of a broad staircase are three portals topped by lights consisting of vertical panes of glass. The vertical stress continues in rows of long windows above a band bearing the name of the school. Over the windows is a segmental molded arch with shield designs above. Two octagonal towers with battlements and long narrow windows flank the entrance. Two small structures on the sides of the staircase served as bicycle rooms. Long narrow windows containing English shields decorate the rooms. The basic form of the building is that of a high central rectangle rising above two wings.

The city's increasing population in the 1920s had necessitated this high school. An architect from Philadelphia, H. Courey Richards,[1] designed it. He used the popular American Jacobethan Revival style. Whiffen's term

Jacobethan succinctly describes the style that derived its forms from English architecture during the reigns of Elizabeth I (1558–1603) and James I (1603–25).[2] The style, as adapted for Jefferson High School, may be recognized by the distinctive use of decoration on windows and gables. Windows tend to be large and rectangular, divided into smaller rectangular panes by stone mullions. Bay windows, or bay effects, are common. Gables rise above the roof in steep triangular forms, and the roof is often flat, with a parapet. Towers and turrets are conspicuous. Tabernacle frames of concrete or cast stone generally enclose the doorways. Brick and stone comprise the usual materials; fine craftsmanship is evident. Educational architecture in America often utilized the Jacobethan style because it evoked the educational excellence and atmosphere of Oxford and Cambridge. Jefferson High School reflects Roanoke's prosperity in the 1920s through its fine use of building materials and the romanticism of its Jacobethan Revival style.

160
Dormitories (known as the Sections)
Roanoke College
College Avenue, Salem
1910

The Jacobethan style was viewed as particularly appropriate for educational buildings because of its English heritage. Using this style, Roanoke College had dormitories designed by Philadelphia architect Frank Rommel in 1910. These buildings were erected by the King Lumber Company of Charlottesville, Virginia.

161
Episcopal Diocesan House
1000 First Street S.W.
Roanoke City
1948

A Jacobethan Revival–style building creates atmosphere for the headquarters of a church organization. The English features of the style are complemented by the use of diamond-pane windows. The stone surrounds of the windows and the door are typical of this style.

162
Hotel Roanoke
19 Jefferson Street N.E., Roanoke City
Begun 1882

The city of Roanoke and the Hotel Roanoke share a common heritage. In 1882, the Atlantic, Mississippi, and Ohio Railroad was reorganized as the Norfolk and Western Railroad, and the town of Big Lick was selected as its headquarters. At the time, Big Lick had about 600 people and about 100 buildings. The town, destined to become one of the nation's important railroad centers, immediately changed its name to Roanoke. Officials of the Roanoke Land and Improvement Company planned a large, elegantly furnished hotel in the tradition of the great English railway hotels, and the Hotel Roanoke was started in 1882,[1] but the present building is the result of many reconstructions. Originally, this English style hotel had thirty-eight rooms, hot and cold running water, an elevator, a call-bell system, and a gaslit dining room with seating for 200 guests.

In the late nineteenth century after the first hotel was completed, an admiring guest wrote:

> Among the buildings which catch the eye of the traveler . . . is the splendid hotel crowning the hill in the midst of lawns, parterres of flowers and ceaseless fountains. Interiorily, the wood-work is hard pine, finished in the natural grain; the furniture ash and cherry and all the arrangements tasteful as well as commodious. The parlor is as pretty a room as you will find in many a mile, and the dining room light and cheerful, with small tables and growing plants. The table and service are of a high order; and I do not know a better resting place for the tourist than this.[2]

After a fire in 1898, the hotel was fully restored in the same style. In 1916 it was enlarged to 180 rooms. In 1931 the northeast wing was rebuilt, and a garage was added. In 1937 the architectural firm of George B. Post and Sons of New York rebuilt the west wing and included a new lobby and dining room. The Cleveland, Ohio, firm of Small, Smith, and Reeb rebuilt the east wing in 1946 and the northeast wing in 1954. Throughout all the renovations the architects maintained the English flavor of the original structure. Today the hotel has about 400 guest rooms, many suites, and a maze of meeting rooms.

The current building has stone facing on the first story, brick on upper stories, and imitation half-timbering on the top level. Hotel Roanoke's roof line forms a distinctive feature of Roanoke's skyline with its gabled dormers and informal massing. The original architects used imitation half-timbering and peaked gables of the nebulous Queen Anne style to add an English feeling, signifying America's love of things in the Old English manner.

Americans often searched for picturesqueness through English forms, with honest treatment of material giving a feeling of welcome and comfort. The Old English domestic manner suited this purpose well, and many of its forms sprang from the architecture of the late medieval, Tudor, and Stuart periods (approximately 1350–1694). Half-timbering, informal massing, and overhanging roofs originated from the medieval vernacular cottage tradition. Real estate agents tend to label the style—sometimes called Cotswold Anglo-Saxon—as Tudor. The materials in Old English are rough stone, stucco, half-timber, and brick. Casement windows or wide bay windows, often attractively grouped, are common. Broad roof surfaces and large English chimneys (the best examples suggest Tudor cluster forms) create continual variety in height. Brick gables and low wall surfaces set off the whole composition. Grander examples have stone or concrete mullioned windows, colorful slate roofs, and carved ornament. The Old English style originally denoted expensive and lavish domestic design done with careful restraint, and large homes in this style dot fashionable suburbs all over the United States. The associations that the Old English has with the nation's Anglo-Saxon, precolonial heritage, make buildings in this style desirable for their charming qualities.

163
Hotel Roanoke
19 Jefferson Street N.E.
Roanoke City
Begun 1882

On a rise above the Norfolk and Western's passenger station, the Hotel Roanoke greeted railroad travelers to the city. Built and rebuilt in the Old English manner (photograph 1931), the hotel is representative of a style usually more typical of suburban residences. Generations of travelers and area residents have used the hotel's numerous facilities. The building continues to be one of the most prominent identifying features of the cityscape of Roanoke.

164
Hotel Roanoke (detail)
19 Jefferson Street N.E.
Roanoke City
Begun 1882

The interior of the main lobby of the Hotel Roanoke continues a tradition of Norfolk and Western Railway hospitality. Wood paneling, upholstered furniture, and many decorative motifs suggest English informality to visitors in this 1945 picture.

165

Old English–Style House
Roanoke Council of Garden
Clubs, Inc.
2713 Avenham Avenue S.W.
Roanoke City
1912

Large massing with symmetrical arrangement of forms indicates the transition from Queen Anne style to a revival style. Here imitation half-timbering and heavy stone at the base are early examples of the use of the Old English style in Roanoke.

166

Old English–Style House
(detail)
Roanoke Council of Garden
Clubs, Inc.
2713 Avenham Avenue S.W.
Roanoke City
1912

Woodiness, often called "honesty," is seen on the inside of Old English houses—continuing the exterior feeling. Machine-cut oak here imitates medieval decoration.

167
**Old English–Style House
1361 Lakewood Drive S.W.
Roanoke City
c. 1920**

Tudor details such as half-timber with bricks and stucco between, various patterns of brick and heavy stone, and a clustered chimney all suggest the late Middle Ages. The Old English style is common to suburbs all over this country, and Roanoke has a number of good examples.

168
**Old English–Style House
4937 Hunting Hills Drive
Roanoke County: Hunting Hills
c. 1970**

The preference for the Old English style continued in suburbia after World War II. The informality of the style—which emphasizes textured shingles, rough plaster, and uneven bricks—continues to be appealing. The half-timbering seen here is nonstructural and purely decorative.

169
**Old English–Style House
4971 Lantern Street, Roanoke
County: North Lakes
1971**

Here imitation half-timbering decorates a suburban split-level house.

170
Bungalow-Style House
2607 Rosalind Avenue S.W., Roanoke City
1922

Built of brick in the bungalow style, the house in figure 170 is one-and-a-
half stories high from the front, and it displays a long, low silhouette with
a distinctive porch. Overhead is a green tile roof in the Japanese manner,
with curved overhanging eaves. The sharp eaved roof and dormers have
knoblike projections accenting their triangular forms. Built in 1922, the
house has an informal air that was considered highly desirable then.

The bungalow style developed in California. The term comes from the
Bengali word *bānglā*—which means a long, low house with a veranda
around it. The term has broader meaning today and refers to a California
style that developed as a reaction to excesses of nineteenth-century revivals and academic traditionalism. The Columbian Exhibition had examples
of the bungalow style at the Chicago World's Fair in 1893. Although the
preponderance of construction at the fair was in a Classical Revival mode,
much attention also focused on the need for simple residences, as economic disturbances in the 1890s had helped create the desire for lower-

cost houses. Visitors at the fair were fascinated with the Japanese display of simple buildings and Louisiana's simple Creole plantation.[1]

The bungalow that evolved after the fair was easy to construct and met the needs of the enormous influx of home buyers into California. Basic features of the new type of house included simple horizontal lines, wide projecting eaves, numerous windows, and one or two large porches. A true bungalow is a small, unassuming, one-story house, often with a dormer or with windows in the gables. Many two-story houses—trying to look like bungalows with a low silhouette—were also built in this basic manner. The style arrived in the east about 1910, by way of publications such as *Bungalow Magazine* and advertisements in popular journals. It became popular throughout the United States, and identical houses in the California mode of design pop up everywhere.

Homeyness and attractiveness without pretention were considered to be the most important qualities of the bungalow. Much of the bungalow's popularity was also due to its relatively low cost. Because the houses were often a single story, the necessity for a stairway and vertical plumbing extensions was eliminated. Outside decoration was plain, and the low forms were considered pleasing in themselves. Bungalows appealed to people desiring informal architectural design and unpretentious, unobstrusive building. Influences on the design range from Indian (Hindustani Caravansary), Bengali, Caribbean, Spanish Colonial, Creole, Japanese, and Swiss to native American barns, log cabins, the Stick and Shingle styles, and Frank Lloyd Wright's Prairie style.[2] The bungalow developed into a truly American architectural form, the ranch house.

171
**Bungalow-Style Houses
2206, 2210, 2214 Wycliffe
Avenue S.W., Roanoke City
c. 1920**

Normally one story—or suggesting one story in its design—the distinctive feature of the bungalow is its broad gable. Structural parts are often displayed frankly, and wood tones were the original preferred colors. Porches are an integral part of the design of this popular style of American house.

Seemingly incongruous in Southwest Virginia, the Spanish house in figure 172 typifies another style popular in the early twentieth century. The local architectural firm of Smithey and Tardy designed the home in 1924, with Mr. Smithey the architect. A red tile roof of low pitch, arches, cast ornament, balconies, iron railings, grills, and other Spanish decorative forms receive asymmetrical treatment. Broad expanses of stuccoed walls separate different elements of the design. The windows vary in size on different elevations and emphasize the informal massing, evoking a Spanish mood.

Starting in Southern California and moving east, the style broadened from the simple Spanish Colonial of the eighteenth and early nineteenth

163

centuries to include direct borrowings from Spain. Always charming and enticing to suburban developers, the style possessed many qualities regarded as beautiful at the time. The Spanish Colonial appealed to people who did not want Old English or American Colonial styles.

In some residential areas of Roanoke these three styles coexist on the same street. Prior to World War II a home buyer could choose among an English country house, an American Colonial manor, or a Spanish ranch. All the forms are vague in their historical associations and are present more as illusion than as direct imitation. The revivals of these styles amounted to little more than a continuation of late nineteenth-century movements. Lingering Victorianism, or the use of symbolism, merely indicates the American craving for decoration to create a picturesque effect. The Spanish Revival house may seem out of place in Roanoke, but its existence here testifies to the nation's continuing interest in past architectural styles.

173
Spanish-Colonial-Revival–Style House
1717 Arlington Road S.W.
Roanoke City
c. 1930
Interrupting a block of bungalows and Colonial Revival houses, this Spanish Revival house comes as a surprise. Textured stucco coating, painted parapet line, and large arches all suggest the Southwest within an unusual context.

174
**Spanish-Colonial-Revival–Style
House
1425 Lafayette Boulevard
N.W., Roanoke City
c. 1930**
Spanish forms are used here to evoke atmosphere. The parapet with a tile border hides a low-pitched roof and adds a further international flavor.

175
**Spanish-Colonial-Revival–Style
House
2501 Kent Avenue S.E.
Roanoke City
1972**
Although incongruous within a residential section of bungalows built in the 1920s and 1930s, this Spanish Revival home was constructed by a couple who had lived in Puerto Rico and in Spain. They purchased a set of plans from a magazine to use as their basic guideline. Rudolph A. Matern of Mineola, N.Y., was the architect, but the owner-builder made many changes because of his interest in creating a Spanish atmosphere.

176
Shenandoah Building
301 First Street S.W., Roanoke City
1911

An early-twentieth-century industrial building constructed of steel and brick, this office building represents a reaction to nineteenth-century decorative excess that pared away ornament and emphasized simple surfaces. Constructed in 1911, it was originally known as the Anchor Building. A tile anchor on the front foyer floor is reminiscent of this. In 1923 the Shenandoah Life Insurance Company bought the building. Four stories were added above the original three stories in 1921 by T. W. Fugate and W. P. Henritze. Decorative details were continued on the top to harmonize with the rest of the building and to unify the structure. Cornices capping off the design are one hallmark of this industrial style. Triple window organization was carried to the cornice, which projects large dentils. Wreaths surround brackets at the junction of every three units. The walls have a skeletal appearance, particularly in the upper four stories. Vertical and horizontal lines are balanced.

Commercial skyscraper building developed in Chicago in the early twentieth century; in fact, this approach to building is often called the Chicago style. Such buildings demonstrate a progressive movement in American architecture. Recognizing American's great wealth and technological achievements, architects saw the need for industrial structures in a noneclectic manner. Functionalism and the utilization of new construction technology were primary requirements of the style.

The Shenandoah Building shows Roanoke's development as an industrial center in the early twentieth century and portrays a style that began to dominate the American scene—a style from which today's modern glass and steel constructions emanated.

177
Railroad Roundhouse
Roanoke City: Shaffers Crossing
1919

The arrival of the Norfolk and Western Railway had turned the small community of Roanoke into a thriving railroad center by 1918. In that year, the Norfolk and Western Railway expanded its operations at Shaffers Crossing with the construction of a roundhouse for the repair and maintenance of locomotives. The design was a standard 115-foot roundhouse. J. P. Pettyjohn and Company constructed the building in sections. Excavations for the first twenty-one stalls began on July 1, 1918. These, along with the 115-foot turntable, started service on September 15, 1919. Between April 1, 1920, and March 18, 1921, another nineteen stalls were added. Today, however, only half of the original forty stalls remain.[1]

For forty years the Shaffers Crossing Roundhouse played an integral part in the Norfolk and Western's steam system. When the railway converted to diesels, the roundhouse needed no structural changes except the addition of high-level platforms and a few fire walls. The Shaffers Crossing Roundhouse now serves diesels as effectively as it once served steam locomotives. Roundhouse stalls have been arranged for a three-spot diesel maintenance system. First, locomotives go to one of two stalls set up for electrical inspection and maintenance work. Then they are moved to the second spot, where they receive necessary mechancial attention. Finally, they are moved to the third spot for cleaning and federal inspection. Intermediate stalls, between spots two and three, are used for six-month and annual maintenance work.

Although over fifty years old, the roundhouse is essentially a modern building because its form is an outgrowth of its functions. Every aspect of the building was planned for efficiency. Even the original wooden truss roof was designed to provide maximum unencumbered space below. The roundhouse has performed the same function for half a century in an industry that has undergone a complete transformation. It seems as much a machine as it is a building!

178
Railroad Shops (main shop)
Campbell Avenue S.E.
Roanoke City
1882–83

The main shop of the Norfolk and Western Railway is located in Roanoke City. Constructed between 1882 and 1883, it was incorporated as the Roanoke Machine Works for building and repairing locomotives and cars. The Machine Works was purchased by the Norfolk and Western in 1897. The Roanoke shops occupy an area of about eighty acres in this picture, circa 1900.

179
Railroad Shops (boiler shop
and erecting shop)
Campbell Avenue S.E.
Roanoke City
1883

Constructed to build and maintain steam engines, this building had a high end-section to enable a full boiler to be lifted into a vertical position. After the disappearance of steam trains, the boiler shop was no longer used for its original purpose, but it continues to be utilized by the railroad.

180
Norfolk and Western Railway General Offices, North Building
8 Jefferson Street N.E., Roanoke City
1931

Decorated in the style called Modernistic, or Art Deco, this office building is outstanding for its ornament—geometric chevrons, zigzags, and hard-edged decoration. A linear, angular composition with a vertical em-

170

phasis is used with stylized decoration. The building steps back, with nine stories in the center, seven in the flanking wings. Surface textures contrast in color; colored, glazed brick occur in abstract patterns. Cut stones surrounding the door contain stylized lettering and decoration, leading the eye upward through bands of yellowish brick offset by patterns of brown brick. A complex design at the roof line emphasizes the skyline. The Modernistic facade facing the Old-English Hotel Roanoke across a small park forms one of the city's finest architectural compositions. The office building cost more than $600,000 and was designed by architects of the Norfolk and Western Railway Company. The contractor, J. P. Pettyjohn and Company of Lynchburg, Virginia, completed the job on September 30, 1931.[1]

An exhibition called the Exposition Internationale des Arts Decoratifs, held in Paris in 1925, gave impetus to this up-to-date style, as well as to its name—Art Deco. Art Deco nurtured the idea that a modern style could be created by means of decoration. The style dealt with surface motifs, zigzags, asymmetry, and any other forms easy to create with a machine. As a style in the 1920s and 1930s, Art Deco stood for French ideas that were modish and expressed with luxurious materials. Simplicity and functionalism gave it immediate appeal. While the vogue for this architectural style did not last very long, it did popularize modern design ideas. Many architects who had been used to adapting past styles abandoned their historical eclecticism for this modern movement. The Norfolk and Western office building demonstrates up-to-date architectural thinking.

181
Walker Apartments
1139 Second Street S.W., Roanoke City
1937

Foreshadowing a new style to come to the valley, the Walker Apartments building used modern materials for structural and expressive purposes. The apartment building, novel for Roanoke in 1937, was (according to local hearsay) "something to be seen on a Sunday afternoon." The Walker Apartments were originally advertised as having air-conditioning (not successful, because the system used air blown over ice, resulting in fogged windows), electric door locks, "Call-up" buttons, telephones in all apartments, and carpeting. The building was constructed of steel beams and cinder blocks, with brick casing on the exterior. Three stories high with a center glass-brick enclosed stairwell in the front, the building has two apartments each on the first and the second floors, and four on the third floor. An outside staircase at the rear leads to balconies and porches on each floor.

Designed by the firm of Frye and Stone of Roanoke and built by contractor Jack Hartman of Roanoke in 1937, the Walker Apartments building is almost devoid of ornament. With the exception of a small decorative panel over the door in what might be called an Art Deco manner, the Walker Apartments building portrays the so-called International style. A flat roof and smooth wall surfaces relieved only by horizontal courses and the horizontal lines in the brick, produce a simple effect. The windows do not have conspicuous frames, and they wrap around the corners of the building. Normal expectation is violated by the freeing of corners from obvious support—a characteristic of many twentieth-century buildings that was made possible by the use of a cantilever. The principal of the cantilever, known for centuries, entails a horizontal structural beam supported at one end and free at the other. Skeleton construction of steel made the cantilever principle practical for carrying upper floors outside the supporting columns.

Flat roof, plain expanses of wall, and cantilever construction pervade in the International style, which rose to prominence in Europe during the 1920s. It was the revolutionary style of the twentieth century. European architects fleeing Nazism brought ideas that transformed American architecture in the 1930s. Modernistic architectural forms with their avant-garde structural and ornamental severity created an architecture in terms of twentieth-century technology. The style's acceptance broke the grip of nineteenth-century historical revivalism on American architecture. This modernism did not represent an architecture based on aesthetics alone, but the style's simple lines and lack of ornament were responses to new economic realities. The Walker Apartments building is an unchanged example of the twentieth century's most influential style.

182
Modernistic-Style Building
124 Kirk Avenue S.W.
Roanoke City
1937

The windows stress verticality on this small building. Their decorative ornaments create effective modern patterns. Contrasting color effects against the flat facade are typical of the Modernistic style, which came to American cities in the 1920s and 1930s.

A Note on Modern Architecture: Post–World War II Buildings

183
Commercial Buildings
Roanoke City
1893–1970s

The structures that follow were chosen to represent the development of modern architecture in the Roanoke Valley. Short factual descriptions are used to indicate some examples of modern styles and technology. Each of the structures stands as a single example of the variety of modern architectural expression.

174

184
Roanoke City Public Library
706 Jefferson Street S.E., Roanoke City
1952

Built of brick and reinforced concrete, this four-story building serves as the downtown library. The exterior walls are of light red brick with limestone trim around the windows. Many of the design ideas reflect the continuation of the International style after World War II. The horizontal quality of the design, the lack of ornament, the asymmetrical organization of volume, and the ribbon windows are features of this style. Designed by the architectural firm of Frantz and Addkison of Roanoke, the building was constructed by general contractor Harry G. Graham of Charlottesville. The library, completed in 1952, can accommodate about 200,000 books, along with various other library services.

185
Community Hospital of Roanoke Valley
101 Elm Avenue S.E., Roanoke City
1965

Situated at the edge of the central business district of Roanoke, the hospital was jointly designed in 1965 by architects Hayes, Seay, Mattern and Mattern of Roanoke, and Skidmore, Owings and Merrill of New York City. Basic Construction Company built the structure. The hospital represents an ingenious solution to the problem of constructing a tall building on a hill. The building consists of ten stories; the first three stories form a forty-foot foundation of precast concrete panels, supporting the upper seven stories. Two stories on the south side are submerged, whereas the same stories on the north side are exposed to provide a podium effect. The fear of nuclear explosions in the 1960s encouraged the planners to provide the hospital with protection from fallout in the submerged south-side levels.

The window walls of the seven-story tower are shaded from direct sunlight by a precast concrete grill that cantilevers out from the fourth floor. This arcaded facade is both functional and visually appealing, as it permits daylight to illuminate the patients' rooms while its horizontal spandrels provide an awning for protection from the sun. The perforated concrete facade also forms a continuous walkway five feet from the glass walls to provide easy access for window cleaning. The overall design of the hospital is that of a high tower set upon a podium.

186
Office Building
1401 Franklin Road S.W., Roanoke City
1967

When this office was built for General Stone and Materials Corporation in 1967, Kenneth L. Motley of Kinsey, Motley and Shane of Roanoke designed it to be an effective advertisement for the corporation's materials. Because the building was situated in a residential area, the architect allowed for grass and open space in his plan, with the result that the building did not substantially alter the character of the neighborhood. Effective landscaping, walks, and a stone screen highlight the entrance.

The company's main stipulation was that the building employ materials they sold. The dominant materials are green serpentine marble and exposed aggregate. For the exterior walls on the first floor, the green serpentine is used in chunks, just as it was quarried. For the interior floors and exterior walks, this same material was crushed to make terrazzo floors. Precast sculptured panels, each with a parabolic motif, sheath the second floor. Their curves play against the straight edges of the boxlike structure. Between the two floors lies a thin strip of windows, which function both to light the first floor offices and to give a floating effect to the second floor.

177

187
Dana Science Building
Hollins College
Route 11, Roanoke County: Hollins
1967

The challenge confronting architects Randolph Frantz and John Chappelear of Roanoke and Douglas Orr, de Cossy, Winder and Associates of New Haven, Connecticut, was to design a structure in a contemporary style, but still harmonizing with a traditional southern woman's college. The result, a building contemporary in simplicity, efficiency, and adaptability to future expansion, was completed in 1967. Enclosing 85,000 square feet, the two-story square structure houses teaching and research facilities for the sciences. Recessed from the center of the first floor to the basement level is a 200-seat auditorium; the overhanging second floor is supported by a series of brick columns and provides a covered walkway.

First-floor walls are floor-to-ceiling glass shielded from the direct sunlight by decorative aluminum grillwork. Two vertical shafts flank each side of the structure to house mechanical equipment. Circular stairways on two sides provide direct access from the outside to the second floor.

The second-floor exterior is a solid brick facade broken only by the shafts and regularly placed slit windows. An open roof court with a domed plexiglass greenhouse is located above the second-floor auditorium. Cantilevered over the court is a concrete astronomy tower.

178

188
James Madison Junior High School
1160 Overland Road S.W., Roanoke City
1970

Located on a distinctive hill site, this school is a good example of functional architecture as applied in the late 1960s and early 1970s. Finished
in October 1970, the brick-and-concrete school complex forms a large
sprawling J over the landscape. Designed by John Chappelear of Roanoke
and built by contractor John W. Daniel, of Danville, Virginia, the school
was an experiment reflecting then-current educational ideals. Windowless
classrooms with removable walls and no doors attempted to open up a
space for educational purposes. Windows only face corridors. Each area of
James Madison School was organized around a different function: offices,
flexible classrooms, cafeteria, and gym.

189
Civic Center of Roanoke City
Orange Avenue and Williamson Road N.W., Roanoke City
1971

From the first planning stages in 1966 until the building was completed in 1971, the Civic Center was envisioned as three separate units: an auditorium (left), a coliseum (right), and an exhibit hall under the outdoor plaza between the two. John Chappelear of Roanoke served as architect and project director. The massive columns seen on the outside of the coliseum express the method of construction. Inverted L-shaped concrete piers are cantilevered forty feet at the top. They hold a steel-truss frame that forms the roof of the structure. Case aggregate panels of bright white stone alternate with cast aggregate panels of light-brown stone to make a foil for the heavy concrete piers.

Inside, a wide corridor encircles the coliseum for efficient traffic flow. Directly off the plaza connecting the coliseum to the theater-auditorium, the entrance lobby of the theater creates a light and airy space. The big white aggregate panels are also used inside the theater as walls. With acoustics as the primary consideration, the architects designed the auditorium to be a great flexible space. The white balcony makes a sculptural form controlled by the requirements of sound: Its underside is an acoustically derived shape, while its extremities flow out into the auditorium, forming a piece of sculpture. The whole complex of auditorium, exhibition hall, and coliseum is a good example of modern technology expressed in the strong, simple shapes of modern architecture.

180

190
Office Building
1315 Franklin Road S.W., Roanoke City
1973

A large space for some 200 employees, this office building was designed to advertise the architectural work of the firm of Hayes, Seay, Mattern and Mattern. Built in 1973, the building is bascially a square box recessed at the bottom, with two stair towers and a service core relieved by horizontal areas of glass and brick spandrels. Tinted glass in recessed strip windows relieves the severe dark-red brick. Built with a structural steel frame and exterior walls of reinforced masonry sheathed with brick, the building has four stories—one of them below ground. Each floor serves a specific function for the architectural firm.

181

191
Norfolk and Western Railway Computer Building
451 Kimball Avenue N.E., Roanoke City
1975

This building houses and protects the computer functions of the Norfolk and Western Railway. Built in 1975 of concrete structural supports with a distinctive brick exterior, it is one of the most unusual industrial buildings in the city. The yellow clay blocks are large—eight inches by eight inches—and are set off by poured concrete that retains its form marks. Holes, surrounding the metal supports for each panel, form part of the design. Emphatically modern in its function as a self-contained computer center, the building is low and sprawling. Thompson, Ventulett and Stainback, Inc., of Atlanta designed the building. H. Hardin Company, also of Atlanta, built it. A central skylight forms the focal point for a two-story-high atrium; the office section encircles this space on the second floor. Separated by thick walls, another section of the building contains the computers, which are protected from fire and vandalism by careful, contemporary space organization.

192
Richard H. Poff Federal Office Building
Franklin Road and First Street S.W., Roanoke City
1975

Finished in 1975 and named after a long-time local Congressional representative and judge, this fourteen-story building added a distinctive form to the Roanoke city skyline. Designed by Hayes, Seay, Mattern and Mattern of Roanoke for the General Services Administration of the United States government, the building utilized a difficult site, while still preserving a few of its trees. Functioning as federal government offices, the building contains approximately 272,000 square feet of office space and a sizable garage. The first floor has post office facilities; the second and third floors house the U.S. district courts. The next ten floors comprise general office space for governmental agencies and rentals. On the fourteenth floor is the building's mechanical equipment. At each side of the building are two service cores built of brownish brick over slip-poured concrete. The central steel and mirror-glass structure is seemingly suspended between these cores, giving a goalpost effect.

193
Antrim Chapel and F. W. Olin Hall, Arts and Humanities Building
Roanoke College
High Street, Salem
1977

With distinctive silhouettes made up of massed broken triangular and trapezoidal forms, these contemporary buildings house Roanoke College's Antrim Chapel, auditorium, stage, and music and art studios. The complex is an attractive addition to modern architecture in Salem. An enclosed courtyard offers space for a small amphitheater. Designed by Vincent G. Kling and Partners of Philadelphia, the chapel was built in 1970 by Watts and Breakell, Inc., of Roanoke, and the arts complex was constructed in 1976–77 by J. M. Turner and Company of Salem.

194
House
3542 Peakwood Drive S.W., Roanoke City
1968

This distinctive house makes a personal statement by the architect, J. M. Yeatts. His contemporary thinking about space for a young family, and his desire for a union of interior and exterior environment created this unusual residence. The cost of outside maintenance was a prime consideration in the design. On the top of a mountain, in a natural setting, the house provides ample entertaining and living space. The low-hanging roof, resembling a mansard, frames the windows, while it appears to flatten the structure. Distinctive peaks allow ventilation into storage space above the living area. Extensive outside living space was one of the few requests the clients made of the architect. Window walls, therefore, dominate the lower-level living room, den, bar, and guest and master bedrooms. Inset patios surround the house and extend to redwood decks. A front door is deeply recessed to provide an outdoor vestibule. The house is one visual unit, with windows, doors, and walls surmounted by the slate roof. Copper strips above each window and doorway form "eyebrows" to divert precipitation. Today the natural materials and textures of the exterior blend with the setting to create one of the most interesting examples of modern architecture in the area.

195
House
Route 688, Roanoke County
1974

Severe geometric shapes distinguish this house. It was designed by architect Timm Jamieson as his own home, and the site stimulated the design of the structure. Instead of relating the site to the structure by the use of indigenous materials—making land and building blend—this house functions as a large piece of sculpture set lightly on the ground. The main living quarters have a superb view and privacy. The street side is closed off and utilities are all hidden within the geometric forms. White sheathing reinforces formal relationships so that the house will not blend into the landscape. Glass walls on the front seem to expand the space inside, as does the careful use of natural light throughout the house. The plan, the elevations, and the geometric forms all flow together in a series of interrelated spaces for living. Reflecting the personality of its designer, this house exudes a strong statement, architecturally and ideologically.

196
Two Houses
733, 723 White Oak Road S.W., Roanoke City
1977, 1977

These two Georgian-style structures emphasize the contemporary New England manner in a continuation of the Colonial Revival style. Details are placed for effect and for associational meaning. No revival has ever assumed more importance to Americans or shown such persistence. The Colonial Revival is everywhere—supermarkets, gas stations, branch banks, churches, business offices. The style has been described as academic, eclectic, antimodern, and even sham decoration—yet it flourishes. Lovers of colonial architecture in our country try to recapture the stylistic coherence of the eighteenth century. To look old and to relate to the eighteenth century are ever-popular American architectural goals. Houses such as these demonstrate vague iconography. The forms may be simple or complex, but they symbolize a nostalgic attempt to recapture an older era. Colonial Revival homes have been degraded as quaint ever since 1890, but they continue to be constructed.

197
Store
6405 Williamson Road, Roanoke County
1976

A rectangular brick structure, decorated on the front by a shake-shingle mansard and situated at the corner of a large parking lot, this building was designed to invite customers inside. According to a local company manager, the design of 7'Eleven stores is basically standard. Corporate architects, local architects, and operations personnel are involved in planning 7'Eleven stores. Here the mansard of cedar shake shingles was used, but the mansard design can also be carried out with red aluminum shingles. This store was constructed between April 14, 1976, and June 25, 1976.

The tacked-on version of the mansard form is popular with fast-food franchises and low-cost building. In no sense are these new mansards structural; they are merely decorative, giving a just-nailed-together effect with precut, purposely crooked shingles. Seemingly related to the revival of crafts, the fake mansard offers a handmade appearance to commercial architecture. The mansard comes from builders unaware of historical forms and concerned only with aesthetic expediency. Ridiculous as they may seem, false mansards have popular appeal. The shake-shingle mansard may be the dominant design mode of the mid-1970s.

198
New Life Temple Pentecostal Holiness Church
5745 Airport Road N.W., Roanoke City
1968

Contemporary religious architecture in the Roanoke area reflects no one specific trend, for both traditional and modern styles are evident. The Grandin Court Baptist Church designed by the firm of Eubank and Caldwell of Roanoke, for example, illustrates a Georgian Revival design. The New Life Temple Pentecostal Holiness Church, designed by the firm of Jarvis and Stoutamire of Roanoke, exemplifies a modern design attitude, with its curved roof and sweeping support for a high cross. Holy Trinity Greek Orthodox Church, also designed by the firm of Jarvis and Stoutamire, takes another modern approach—its arched colonnades project a contemporary, yet Mediterranean image that restyles old shapes for ornament. These churches all expressed historically established symbols in terms of modern culture.

199
Grandin Court Baptist Church
2660 Brambleton Avenue S.W.
Roanoke City
1967

200
Holy Trinity Greek Orthodox
Church
30 Huntington Boulevard N.E.
Roanoke City
1965

201
Mobile Home
Ramey's Mobile Home Park
1600 Lynchburg Turnpike, Salem
1969

Low-cost housing in the Roanoke Valley is, in part, represented by many mobile homes scattered throughout the area. A mobile home may be defined as a movable unit constructed on its own frame and designed without a permanent foundation. The majority of these structures are transported to a site supplied with utility hookups, and there they remain with the base enclosed and porches added. Mobile homes play an essential role in low-cost housing. Prefabricated construction reduces the price, which usually includes all appliances and furnishings. The exterior of a mobile home presents certain problems. In order to maintain the mobility of the home, a basic size for transportation cannot be violated. All kinds of plastic embellishments—grained wood siding, stone or brick veneer, shingle mansards, and various colonial motifs—make mobile homes more acceptably houselike today.

202
Housing Development
Tampa Drive and Orlando Avenue, Roanoke County: Sun Valley
1962–69

The average developer's residential unit in the 1960s was a single house of approximately 1200 square feet placed on a lot that was about 60 feet wide and 120 feet deep. The typical house was set back some 25 feet from the sidewalk and was about 10 feet from each of the sidelines of the property. House after house, row after row, subdivision adjoining subdivision, suburbia sprawled. From coast to coast the process repeated itself. Sometimes two or three catalog styles were alternated, but basically, each house, and each street, was identical to the next. The federal government, through the Federal Housing Administration and other agencies, attempted to deal with serious housing shortages after World War II and imposed restrictions on the building industry. Suburbia today is enmeshed in conflicting interests. The home-building industry, manufacturers of building supplies, government officials, banks, and savings and loan institutions make thousands of separate decisions with little or no relationship to one another, and with little regard to the future. Although called inefficient, ugly, and oppressive by critics, developments are still home for millions of Americans who find their expectations fulfilled by this kind of housing.

203
Shopping Center
Crossroads Mall
Williamson, Hershberger, and Airport roads N.W., Roanoke City
1961

In the mid-1950s a new business concept for suburbs developed. The idea that shopping centers would serve as mercantile cores provided strong competition for the old inner-city stores. Close-to-home location, free parking, and evening shopping hours attracted customers to the shopping centers. Sociologists claim that many of these centers provide a focal point and a symbol of identity for the otherwise formless sprawl of suburbia.

Crossroads Mall, located at the northern edge of Roanoke City on twenty-five acres, was one of Virginia's first shopping centers with a completely enclosed, air-conditioned mall. T. A. Carter, Jr., and T. D. Steele, Roanoke developers, worked out the design after they had studied several different shopping centers throughout the country. H. A. Lucas and Sons of Roanoke was general contractor.

The main building complex covers 248,000 square feet of usable space and is surrounded by extensive parking areas. Finished in 1961, the main building is constructed of a steel frame with stone, brick, and glass. The axis of the building is a mall connected to the outside parking area by three corridors. Every store has an entrance or corridor onto the mall and some have outside entrances as well. The interior is landscaped and decorated with plants and fountains; there are kiosks, benches for weary shoppers, and piped-in music. Auto-service buildings are adjacent to the parking lots, along with a theater–office building, a small row of other businesses, and a grocery store–drug store complex.

204
Star
Mill Mountain Park
Roanoke City
1949

Roanoke, like some other Virginia cities, is endowed with an architectural landmark. Charlottesville has the Rotunda, Richmond has the State Capitol, Lynchburg has Monument Terrace, and Roanoke has a star—a tremendous one on Mill Mountain—proclaiming that the city is the "Star City of the South." Whether the star is architecture might legitimately be argued. Architecture or not, however, it was the largest man-made, illuminated star in the world according to publicity at the time it was built. Cosponsored by the Roanoke Merchants Association and the Chamber of Commerce, it was built with $27,000 collected from local businessmen. The Roy C. Kinsey Sign Company of Roanoke designed and erected the star.

Standing at the top of Mill Mountain, which rises more than 800 feet above the city, the star was a monumental undertaking—using 500,000 pounds of concrete and 60,000 pounds of steel to support a 10,000 pound steel star mounted on a hundred-foot steel tower. The construction is as tall as an eight-story building. Two thousand feet of neon tubing manufactured by the Corning Glass Works make the lighted star visible for ten to fifteen miles from the ground and for some sixty miles from the air.

The ceremonial lighting of the star with white neon tubing on Thanksgiving eve, November 23, 1949, received national publicity. Originally the star was to be lighted only for holidays and special events, but the display proved so popular that it now shines every night of the year. For several years the star was lighted with red tubing for twenty-four hours after a local traffic death, to remind people to drive carefully, but that practice has been abated. Continuing its monumental, commemorative function for the city, the star was lighted in red, white, and blue during the bicentennial celebrations.

205
Six Mile Strip
Williamson Road, Roanoke City and Roanoke County
1970s

Strip architecture accepts and uses the economic conditions of the time. The buildings along Williamson Road, for instance, achieve symbolic effects through the use of direct visual attraction rather than by abstract decoration. The new architectural vernacular, urban sprawl, came to stay in the 1970s, but this development of our main arteries may have created visual pollution. Nonetheless, the chaotic juxtaposition of small businesses and fast-food shops has vitality. Each building and each sign is designed to create specific reponses from the viewer through the use of instantly recognizable symbols, which often reside in the decoration of the structure itself. Architectural writers call these buildings decorated sheds, but they are powerfully expressive. Imagery abounds to create that one special atmosphere for that particular restaurant, fast-service store, or other business. The symbolism of these buildings serves to identify the individual offering. One can see Cape Cod, French Provincial, Dutch Colonial, Miami Beach Modern, or Shake-Shingle Mansard, each one enclosing interiors of great efficiency. The universal pop-culture imagery—McDonald's yellow arches are the most familiar—offers the comfort of recognition as well as the hamburger.

From the Roanoke Civic Center to Hollins College, the six-mile strip is a shopping center for the automobile. The cacophony of signs and drive-in facilities all beckon the driver. Highly diversified and unplanned, the strip development embodies commercial expression. Its advertising is successful. Ugly and unpleasant to some viewers, this exhibitionistic architecture may excite others. Divorced from the residential community, the strip culture spreads continually in response to the accelerated pace and mobility of the twentieth century.

197

Acknowledgments
Illustration Credits
Notes
Bibliography
Index

Acknowledgments

Without the help of many people, this project would not have been possible. Thanks to the Katherine Nelson Fishburn Foundation and the Hollins College faculty-administered Carnegie-Mellon fund for support. Our capable editor Lynn Davis offered excellent criticism. Particular thanks for their insights into local history go to Jean Showalter and Kyle Shelor.

In local libraries we had invaluable assistance. Shirley Henn and Mildred Mitchell at Hollins College Library, Carol Tuckwiller at the Virginia Room of the Roanoke City Public Library, and Sue Williams at the library of the *Roanoke Times and World-News* were all very helpful. In local courthouses the personnel of the Office of the Clerk of the courts for Botetourt County, Montgomery County, Roanoke City, and Roanoke County gave kindly guidance. Likewise, Jim Fulghum, Joe Logan, and Phil Lemon helped with legal problems. Dorothy McCauley Butler generously shared her family letter, and Helen Cobb and J. J. Cobb permitted reproduction of their painting of Salem.

Architects Timm Jamieson and Eldon Karr gave opinions about local buildings. The 1958 surveys by architectural student Waller Hunt saved us much time.

Roanoke Valley Historical Society workers Sallie Brown, David Chrisman, Caroline Hoppe, Donna Ware, and Julie Wheeler helped in a variety of ways.

Many Hollins College students combined classroom work and fieldwork to contribute to this study. Students' findings have been utilized throughout our work. Acknowledgment is given to Bryding Adams, Ann Aptaker, Kathy Barger, Anne Baskerville, Ann Bedell, Denise Bethel, Anne Blazy, Mary Ann Brockenborough, Lucy Chappell, Elizabeth Cheek, Ellen Cluett, Nancy Dize, Lindy Eubanks, Clair Fahnestock, Anne Foreman, Wendy French, Sandy Gubb, Paula Haff, Carey Hazlegrove, Isabel Hill, Pat Hooker, Kitty Hutcheson, Nancy Ireland, Mary Stuart Johnson, Elizabeth Jones, Mary Bess Keiser, Luci Shaw Kincanon, Helen Lewis, Catherine McConnell, Milly McGehee, Missy McKeon, Betsy Manley, Susan Martin, Louisa Meacham, Anne Merritt, Sarah Morten, Olivia Motch, Page Murrell, Anne Parker, Dale Pierce, Tricia Rawls, Diana Reuter, Nancy Rogers, Linda Scott, Ruth Selden, Elizabeth Sellars, Jane Smith, Mary Yancey Spencer, Julie Stinnett, Cinder Talcott, Gregory Weidman, Becky Wheeler, Dale Woods, Robin Woody.

Special thanks for encouragement, contributions, and stimulation are due to Charles T. Burton, genealogist; Calder Loth, Senior Architectural Historian, Virginia Historic Landmarks Commission; Frances J. Niederer, Professor of Art, Hollins College; Lewis M. Phelps, Director of Public Relations and Advertising, Norfolk and Western Railway.

Three grants from the Mellon-Ford Fund administered by Hollins College made much of our work possible.

Finally, particular thanks to our tireless typists: Kathy Winborne, Nancy Moomaw, Eileen Montgomery, Terry Cavandish, Diane Lynn, and Betty Sumpter. Artists Doug Trent and Susan Winborne added greatly to our presentation.

Illustration Credits

Figs. 1 (accession number 78.301.1), 4 (accession number 78.301.1): courtesy of Abby Aldrich Rockefeller Folk Art Center, Williamsburg, Virginia

Figs. 2, 125, 131, 134, 135–36 (Wayne Deel), 141, 155, 160, 189, 203, 204: courtesy of *Roanoke Times and World News*

Figs. 3, 5, 15, 50, 51, 52, 54, 56, 71, 73, 100, 104, 115, 124, 127, 184: photographs by Roger M. Winborne, Jr.

Figs. 6, 9, 31, 53, 82: drawings by Susan L. Winborne

Figs. 7, 11, 12, 13, 22, 57: photographs by Cary Hazlegrove

Figs. 8, 14, 16, 17, 18, 19, 20, 24, 25, 34, 35, 39, 43, 45, 46, 49, 59, 62, 68, 69, 70, 72, 75, 76, 77, 79, 86, 87, 99, 105, 106, 111, 114, 118, 123, 126, 128, 130, 132, 137, 140, 161, 168, 173, 174, 175, 183, 188, 195, 196, 197, 199, 200: photographs by Judith Farb

Figs. 10, 21, 74, 80, 144, 148: photographs by Milly McGehee

Figs. 23, 27, 32, 36, 37, 38, 40, 41, 42, 44, 47, 48, 55, 58, 81, 83, 84, 85, 93, 94, 102, 103, 107, 110, 116, 121, 122, 142, 145, 151, 152, 153, 158, 165, 167, 169, 171, 172, 181, 182, 198: photographs by Sky Preece

Figs. 26, 33, 67, 101, 108, 112, 113, 149, 157, 159, 170, 176, 177, 185, 186, 194, 201, 202: photographs by Nancy Dize

Figs. 28, 29, 63, 64, 66, 90, 91, 109, 117, 129, 138, 139, 150, 166, 205: photographs by Bob Sulkin

Figs. 30, 143: courtesy of The Roanoke Valley Historical Society

Figs. 60, 61, 119, 120, 162, 163, 164, 178, 179, 180, 191: courtesy of the Norfolk and Western Railway

Figs. 65, 78, 154: photographs by Jane Smith

Figs. 88, 89, 92, 95, 96, 187: courtesy of Hollins College

Figs. 97, 98, 193: courtesy of Roanoke College

Fig. 133: courtesy of *Roanoker* magazine

Figs. 146, 147: photographs by Lewis Phelps

Fig. 156: photograph by Mary Stuart Johnson

Figs. 190, 192: courtesy of Hayes, Seay, Mattern and Mattern

Notes

Introduction

1 Herbert P. Woodward, *Geology and Mineral Resources of the Roanoke Area, Virginia*, p. 3.

2 Ibid., p. 3.

3 Ibid., p. 1.

4 N. K. Breeding, Jr., and J. W. Dawson, *Roanoke County Groundwater*, p. 11.

5 Woodward, *Geology*, p. 1.

6 F. B. Kegley, *Kegley's Virginia Frontier*, p. 524.

7 Rev. Wm. J. Hinke and Charles E. Kemper, eds., "Moravian Diaries of Travels through Virginia: Diary of the Journey of the First Colony of Single Brethren to North Carolina, Oct. 8–Nov. 17, 1753," p. 151.

8 Luci Shaw Kincanon, "Roanoke County Barns of the Nineteenth Century," p. 14.

9 Rev. Wm. J. Hinke and Charles E. Kemper, eds., "Moravian Diaries of Travels through Virginia: Extracts from the Diary of Leonhard Schnell and John Brandmueller of Their Journey to Virginia, Oct. 12–Dec. 12, 1749," pp. 122–26.

10 Ibid., pp. 123–25.

11 Hinke and Kemper, eds., "Moravian Diaries: Journey of the First Colony," p. 272.

12 Margaret Scott, "Thomas and Tasker Tosh," p. 6.

13 Kegley, *Kegley's Virginia Frontier*, pp. 96 et seq.

14 Ibid., p. 58.

15 "A map of the British Colonies in North America with the Roads, Distances, Limits, and Extent of the settlements, Humbly inscribed to the Right Honourable the Earl of Halifax By Jn. Mitchell. Published by the author 1755," listed in *1776: The British Story of the American Revolution*, item 576. Map size: 197 cm. × 144 cm. (76.83″ × 56.16″); British Museum reference: K. 118d. 26 (K. top. CXVIII 49. b).

16 Writers' Program of the Works Projects Administration in the State of Virginia, *Roanoke: Story of City and County*, p. 79.

17 Joseph Martin, *A New and Comprehensive Gazetteer of Virginia*, p. 233.

18 Henry Howe, *Historical Collections of Virginia*, p. 447.

19 Martin, *Gazetteer*, p. 328.

20 See Helen Lewis, "What They Owned in the 1840s."

21 Howe, *Historical Collections of Virginia*, pp. 447–48.

22 Arthur M. Bixby (historian, Roanoke Chapter NRHS), "Area Rail History Set Straight," *Roanoke Times and World-News*, Wednesday, June 11, 1980, p. A-8.

23 William McCauley, ed., *History of Roanoke County, Salem, Roanoke City, Virginia and Representative Citizens*, p. 152.

24 James A. Pugh and Charles I. Stewart, "Roanoke City, Virginia," pp. 94–95.

25 Raymond P. Barnes, *A History of Roanoke*, p. 120. The 1883 date for this quotation appears in "Roanoke: 'Star City' Rose from Rough, Bawdy Past" by Ben Beagle in *Roanoke Times and World-News*, Sunday, August 12, 1979, p. DRV-60.

26 McCauley, *History of Roanoke*, p. 159.

27 *Salem, Virginia: Its Advantages and Attractions*.

28 J. H. Chataigne, comp., *Chataigne's Virginia Gazetteer and Classified Business Directory, 1893–94*, p. 1080.

Rectangular Log Cabin

1 Henry Glassie, "A Central Chimney Continental Log House," p. 34.

2 Henry Glassie, "The Types of the Southern Mountain Cabin," Appendix C in *The Study of American Folklore: An Introduction*, ed. Jan Harold Brunvand, p. 347.

3 F. B. Kegley, *Kegley's Virginia Frontier*, p. 190.

4 Glassie, "Southern Mountain Cabin," p. 345.

5 Davyd Foard Hood, "The Architecture of the New River Valley," in *Carolina Dwelling: The Student Publication of the School of Design*, ed. Doug Swaim, 26:206.

6 Royster Lyle, Jr., and Pamela Hemenway Simpson, *The Architecture of Historic Lexington*, p. 295.

7 Glassie, "Southern Mountain Cabin," p. 355.

Square Log Cabin

1 Henry Glassie, "The Types of the Southern Mountain Cabin," Appendix C in *The Study of American Folklore: An Introduction*, ed. Jan Harold Brunvand, p. 351.

2 Rev. Wm. J. Hinke and Charles E. Kemper, eds., "Moravian Diaries of Travels through Virginia: Extracts from the Diary of Leonhard Schnell and John Brandmueller of Their Journey to Virginia, Oct. 12–Dec. 12, 1749," p. 122.

Single-Crib Barn

1 Henry Glassie, "The Variation of Concepts within Tradition: Barn Building in Otsego County, New York," p. 177.

Double-Crib Barn

1 For this idea and many of the facts that follow see Luci Shaw Kincanon, "Roanoke County Barns of the Nineteenth Century."

2 See John Fitchen, *The New World Dutch Barn: A Study of Its Characteristics, Its Structural System, and Its Probable Erection Procedures*, p. 136, drawing 17, and Henry Glassie, "The Variation of Concepts within Tradition: Barn Building in Otsego County, New York," p. 223, text figure 61a.

Bake Oven

1 See Henry Glassie, *Pattern in the Material Folk Culture of the Eastern United States*, pp. 8, 9, 10, 36, 41, 42; Amos Long, Jr., "Bakeovens in the Pennsylvania Folk-Culture," and Amos Long, Jr., "Outdoor Bakeovens in Berks."

Overhang Outbuilding

1 Henry Glassie, *Pattern in the Material Folk Culture of the Eastern United States*, pp. 8–9.

Tobacco Barn

1 W. H. Snow, *Snow's Modern Barn System of Raising and Curing Tobacco*, pp. 11–12.

2 John Fraser Hart, "The Character of Tobacco Barns and Their Role in the Tobacco Economy of the U.S."

3 Henry Howe, *Historical Collections of Virginia*, pp. 160–62.

Stone House

1 Deed Book 5, p. 26, Botetourt County Courthouse, Fincastle, Va.

2 "List of Land Tax District of Hugh Allen, Botetourt County," in Land Book 1798, Botetourt County, Botetourt County Courthouse, Fincastle, Va.; listed under Samuel Harshberger.

3 Writers' Program of the Works Progress Administration in the State of Virginia, *Roanoke: Story of City and County*, p. 55.

I-Form House

1 Inventory, Appraisements, and Sales Book 1, p. 89, Roanoke County Courthouse, Salem, Va.

2 Henry Glassie, *Folk Housing in Middle Virginia*, p. 171.

3 W. L. Whitwell and Lee W. Winborne, "The Sedon Journal," p. 8. The old account book in which Sedon kept his journal is now in the archives of the Roanoke Valley Historical Society, Roanoke, Va.

4 Grace Pierce Heffelfinger, "The I House: An Architectural Form in Rockbridge County, Virginia," p. 15.

5 "List of land tax within the district of James McClanahan, Commissioner, in the County of Botetourt for the year 1831," in Botetourt County Land Book, 1831, Botetourt County Courthouse, Fincastle, Va.; listed under Lewis Harvey.

6 Inventory, Appraisements, and Sales Book 1, p. 104, Roanoke County Courthouse, Salem, Va.

7 See Whitwell and Winborne, "The Sedon Journal," pp. 1–27.

Hall-and-Parlor House

1 Ruth Little-Stokes, "The North Carolina Porch: A Climatic and Cultural Buffer," in *Carolina Dwelling: The Student Publication of the School of Design*, ed. Doug Swaim, 26:109.

2 Interview with Kyle Shelor, March 15, 1979.

3 Henry Glassie, *Pattern in the Material Folk Culture of the Eastern United States*, p. 81.

4 Shelor interview.

5 Robert Keber, "Site Selection of Pre-1940 Mountain Houses," in *Carolina Dwelling*, ed. Swaim, 26:196–201.

6 Ibid., p. 198.

7 R. G. Collingwood and J. N. L. Myres, *Roman Britain and the English Settlements*, p. 217.

8 Keber, "Site Selection," p. 198.

9 "A list of the land tax within the district of William Wade, commissioner of the revenue in Montgomery County for the year 1835," in Land Books, 1832–37, Montgomery County, p. 21, Montgomery County Courthouse, Christiansburg, Va.; listed under George Surface, Jr.

10 "A list of the lands within the Eastern district of Montgomery County—[illegible] by Wm. Wade—[illegible] for 1837," in Land Books, 1832–37, Montgomery County, n.p., Montgomery County Courthouse, Christiansburg, Va.; listed under George Surface, Jr.

11 Deed Book O, pp. 373–74, Montgomery County Courthouse, Christiansburg, Va.

12 Deed Book D, p. 62, Roanoke County Courthouse, Salem, Va.

13 "List of the Land within the District of C. H. Heff, Assessor for the County of Roanoke in the Year 1850," in Land Book, 1845–1869, Roanoke County, p. 15, Roanoke County Courthouse, Salem, Va.

14 Inventory, Appraisements, and Sales, Book no. 6, p. 265, Roanoke County Courthouse, Salem, Va.

15 Helen Lewis, "What They Owned in the 1840s," p. 41.

Spring Resort Buildings

1 Edward A. Pollard, *The Virginia Tourist: Sketches of the Springs and Mountains of Virginia*, p. 27.

2 *Description of the Album of Virginia: or the Old Dominion, Illustrated*, fig. 44.

3 William McCauley, ed., *History of Roanoke County, Salem, Roanoke City, Virginia, and Representative Citizens*, p. 320.

4 J. J. Moorman, M.D., *Mineral Springs of North America: How to Reach and How to Use Them*, p. 164.

5 Ibid.

6 *Tourists and Excursionists Guide Book: Summer Homes*, pp. 52–53.

7 Ibid., p. 52.

8 Ibid.

9 Ibid., p. 53.

10 R. Lewis Wright, "Edward Beyer and the Album of Virginia," p. 37.

Monterey

1 See note 1 and accompanying text for "Hall-and-Parlor House," above.

2 "List of the Land Tax within the District of J. R. C. Brown, Jr., Commissioner of the Revenue in the County of Roanoke for the Year 1846," in Land Book, 1845–1860, Roanoke County, p. 16, Roanoke County Courthouse, Salem, Va.

3 Inventory, Appraisements, and Sales, Book 2, p. 329, Roanoke County Courthouse, Salem, Va.

4 Will Book 1, p. 65, Roanoke County Courthouse, Salem, Va.

5 Inventory, Appraisements, and Sales, Book 3, pp. 197–99, Roanoke County Courthouse, Salem, Va.

6 See Inventory, Appraisements, and Sales, Book 3, p. 226, Roanoke County Courthouse, Salem, Va.; Raymond Barnes, "Monterey," *Roanoke World News*, April 28, 1962, p. 6; Writer's Program of the Works Progress

Administration in the State of Virginia, *Roanoke: Story of City and County*, p. 334.

Belle Aire

1 "List of the land within the District of C. H. Houff, Assessor for the County of Roanoke in the Year 1850," in Land Book, 1845–1860, Roanoke County, p. 22, Roanoke County Courthouse, Salem, Va.; listed under Madison Pitzer.

2 W. L. Whitwell and Lee W. Winborne, "The Sedon Journal," p. 15.

Salem Presbyterian Church

1 Letter from William McCauley to James McCauley, March 14, 1866; in possession of Dorothy McCauley Butler, Salem, Va.

2 Archives, Salem Presbyterian Church, Salem, Va.

3 Ibid.

4 Ibid.

Williams-Brown House-Store

1 William McCauley, ed., *History of Roanoke County, Salem, Roanoke City, Virginia, and Representative Citizens*, p. 300.

2 Chancery file no. 277, Roanoke County Courthouse, Salem, Va.

3 McCauley, ed., *History of Roanoke County*, p. 300.

4 Vertical file, "Buildings in County," Roanoke County Courthouse, Salem, Va.

5 Common Law Order Book D, p. 415, Roanoke County Courthouse, Salem, Va.; Anne Lowry Worrell, comp., *Over the Mountain Men: Their Early Court Records in Southwest Virginia*, p. 69; correspondence from Charles T. Burton, genealogist, to the authors, May 9, 1978.

6 McCauley, *History of Roanoke County*, p. 300.

7 Deed Book E, pp. 204, 206, Roanoke County Courthouse, Salem, Va.

8 Vertical file, "Buildings in County," Roanoke County Courthouse, Salem, Va.

9 "List of the Land Tax within the District of Joshua R. C. Brown, Jr., Commissioner of the Revenue in the County of Roanoke for the Year 1845," in Landbook, 1845–1860, Roanoke County, p. 24, Roanoke County Courthouse, Salem, Va.; listed under William C. Williams.

10 "List of the Taxable Town Lots within the District of J. R. C. Brown, Jr., Commissioner of the Revenue in the County of Roanoke for the Year 1846," in Landbook, 1845–1860, Roanoke County, p. 28, Roanoke County Courthouse, Salem, Va.; listed under William C. Williams.

11 "List of the Taxable Town Lots within the District of A. L. Pitzer, Commissioner of the Revenue in the County of Roanoke for the Year 1845," in Landbook, 1851–1855, Roanoke County, p. 38, Roanoke County Courthouse, Salem, Va.; listed under William C. Williams' Heirs.

12 Inventory, Appraisements, and Sales, Book 3, p. 130, Roanoke County Courthouse, Salem, Va.

13 Vertical file W-1, voucher no. 112, Roanoke County Courthouse, Salem, Va.

14 Ibid.

15 Ibid.

16 Ibid.

17 Vertical file, "Buildings in County," Roanoke County Courthouse.

Benjamin Deyerle Place

1 "List of the Land Tax within the District of Andrew L. Pitzer, Commissioner of Revenue in the County of Roanoke for the Year 1853," in Land Book, 1851–55, Roanoke County, p. 8, Roanoke County Courthouse, Salem, Va.

2 Fred Fisher, "Rev. P. M. Lewis, Born a Slave in Virginia, Passes His Eighty-fifth Birthday," *Waterloo* (Iowa) *Courier*, March 8, 1934.

3 "Rev. Peyton M. Lewis, Slave, Teacher, Preacher," *Journal of the Roanoke Historical Society* 7, no. 2 (1971):51.

4 Ibid.

5 Ibid.

Pleasant Grove

1 "List of the Land Tax within the District of A. Pitzer, Commissioner of the Revenue in the County of Roanoke for the Year 1854," in Land Book, 1851–55, Roanoke County, p. 8, Roanoke County Courthouse, Salem, Va.

2 See W. L. Whitwell and Lee W. Winborne, "The Sedon Journal."

3 Ibid., pp. 12–13.

Buena Vista

1 Deed Book 15, p. 480, Botetourt County Courthouse, Fincastle, Va.

2 "List of the Land Tax within the District of James McClanahan, Commissioner in the County of Botetourt for the Year 1823," in Land Tax Book, 1820–1826, Botetourt County, reel 40, Botetourt County Courthouse, Fincastle, Va.; Botetourt County Land Book 1824 C, p. 23; listed under William Langhorne.

3 "[Missing] Commissioner in the County of Botetourt for the Year 1826," in Land Tax Book, 1820–1826, Botetourt County, reel 40, Botetourt County Courthouse, Fincastle, Va.; Botetourt County Land Book 1826 C, p. 25; listed under William Langhorne.

4 Deed Book 20, p. 67, Botetourt County Courthouse, Fincastle, Va. This deed was dated January 4, 1833. The deed was also recorded August 31, 1845: Deed Book C, p. 42, Roanoke County Courthouse, Salem, Va.

5 Ibid.

6 "List of the Land Tax within the District of J. R. C. Brown, Jr., Commissioner of the Revenue in the County of Roanoke for the Year 1847," in Land Book, 1845–1860, Roanoke County, p. 23, Roanoke County Courthouse, Salem, Va.

7 "Assessment of Lands, 1840," in Reassessment Land Books, 1840, 1861–63, Roanoke County, p. 12, Roanoke County Courthouse, Salem, Va.

8 "List of the Land within the District of P. H. Houff, Assessor for the County of Roanoke in the Year 1850," in Land Book, 1845–1860, Roanoke County, p. 28, Roanoke County Courthouse, Salem, Va.

9 John S. Wise, *The End of an Era*, p. 221.

10 "Table of Tracts of Land for the Year 1892 in Roanoke County, in Big Lick District, D. E. Kefauver, Commissioner of Revenue," in Land Book, 1892–1893, Roanoke County, p. 17, Roanoke County Courthouse, Salem, Va.

11 Deed Book 5, p. 519, Roanoke County Courthouse, Salem, Va.

12 Deed Book 620, p. 486, Roanoke City Courthouse, Roanoke, Va.

West Domitory, Hollins College

1 W. H. Walsh, comp., *Walsh's Roanoke, Virginia, City Directory for 1900*, p. 113.

2 *Ledger for the years 1898–99, 1899–1900, 1900–1901 A*, p. 657, Hollins College Archives, Fishburn Library, Hollins College, Va.

3 Frances J. Niederer, *Hollins College: An Illustrated History*, p. 44.

East Dormitory, Hollins College

1 Frances J. Niederer, *Hollins College: An Illustrated History*, p. 20.

2 Ibid., p. 23.

3 Minutes of the Board of Trustees, March 5, 1856, Hollins College Archives, Fishburn Library, Hollins College, Va.

4 Niederer, *Hollins College*, p. 23.

5 Ibid., p. 20.

Main Building, Hollins College

1 Frances J. Niederer, *Hollins College: An Illustrated History*, p. 25.

2 See W. L. Whitwell and Lee W. Winborne, "The Sedon Journal."

Bradley Hall, Hollins College

1 Frances J. Niederer, *Hollins College: An Illustrated History*, p. 31.

Botetourt Dining Hall, Hollins College

1 Frances J. Niederer, *Hollins College: An Illustrated History*, p. 39.

2 Ibid.

Roanoke College, Main College Complex

1 Writers' Program of the Works Progress Administration in the State of Virginia, *Roanoke: Story of City and County*, p. 271.

2 William Edward Eisenberg, *The First Hundred Years: Roanoke College, 1842–1942*, pp. 45–46, 199.

3 Ibid., pp. 192–93.

4 Ibid., pp. 84–85, 118–19.

Bittle Hall, Roanoke College

1 William Edward Eisenberg, *The First Hundred Years: Roanoke College, 1842–1942*, pp. 149, 154.

2 Ibid., p. 149.

3 Andrew Boyd and Co., comp., *Virginia State Business Directory, 1871–72*, pp. 194, 208.

4 J. H. Chataigne, comp., *Chataigne's Virginia Gazetteer and Classified Business Directory, 1884–'5*, p. 547.

5 Archives, Salem Presbyterian Church, Salem, Va.

Johnsville Meetinghouse

1 Eliza Davidson, "North Carolina Country Churches: Explorations in the Mountains and the Tidewater," *Carolina Dwelling: The Student Publication of the School of Design*, ed. Doug Swaim, 26:189.

2 This and other facts in this paragraph were provided in an interview with William C. Brunk, minister, July 19, 1978.

Nineteenth-Century Storefronts

1 J. H. Chataigne, comp., *Chataigne's Virginia Gazetteer and Classified Business Directory, 1893–94*, p. 1080.

Right-Angle House

1 Deed Book 19, p. 555, Roanoke County Courthouse, Salem, Va.

Second Empire–Style House

1 "Table of Town Lots for the Year 1882 in Roanoke County, in Salem District, Geo. H. Landon, Commissioner of the Revenue," Land Book, 1881–1883, Roanoke County, p. 3, no. 25, Roanoke County Courthouse, Salem, Va.

2 "Table of Town Lots for the Year 1883 in Roanoke County, in Salem District, Geo. H. Landon, Commissioner of the Revenue," Land Book, 1881–1883, Roanoke County, no. 34, Roanoke County Courthouse, Salem, Va.

Administration Building, Hollins College

1 Frances J. Niederer, *Hollins College: An Illustrated History*, p. 76.

Roanoke City Municipal Building

1 *Roanoke, Virginia, Directory: 1913* (Roanoke, Va.: Hill Directory Company, 1913), 1:300.

Renaissance Revival–Style House

1 Sara Boggs Bemiller, "Magnifico: Italian Splendor on a Hill in South Roanoke," p. 36.

Firehouse no. 1

1 Raymond P. Barnes, *A History of Roanoke*, p. 420.

2 Cronin Minton, "Progress Closing in on Fire Station no. 1," *Roanoke Times*, Sunday, November 1, 1970, p. C-8. "Firemen Are in New Quarters," *Roanoke Times*, Wednesday, February 6, 1907, p. 5.

3 See John Maass, "Architecture and Americanism: Or Pastiches of Independence Hall," pp. 17–25.

4 William B. Rhoads, *The Colonial Revival*, vol. 1, p. xxxvii.

5 Ibid., p. 379.

6 Ibid., pp. 392–93.

7 See Norma Lugar, "The Tragic Genius of Robert Allen."

8 Sinclair Lewis, *Babbitt*, quoted in Alan Gowans, *Architecture in New Jersey: A Record of American Civilization*, p. 111.

9 See Rhoads, *The Colonial Revival*, 1:431.

10 Ibid., p. 461.

St. Andrew's Roman Catholic Church

1 For this fact and many of those that follow, see W. L. Whitwell, "Saint Andrew's Roman Catholic Church: Roanoke's High Victorian Gothic Landmark."

First Presbyterian Church

1 This fact and many of those that follow were found in the archives of the First Presbyterian Church, Roanoke, Va.

Jefferson High School

1 Roanoke City Archives, Municipal Building, Roanoke, Va.

2 Marcus Whiffen, *American Architecture since 1780*, p. 179.

Hotel Roanoke

1 This fact and many of those that follow were found in the archives of the Norfolk and Western Railway Company, Roanoke, Va.

2 "Hotel Roanoke Celebrates: The Completion of a New $225,000 Addition," *Norfolk and Western Magazine* 9, no. 12 (December 1931):697.

Bungalow-Style House

1 Clay Lancaster, "The American Bungalow."

2 Ibid., p. 252.

Railroad Roundhouse

1 This fact and those that follow were found in the archives of the Norfolk and Western Railway Company, Roanoke, Va.

Norfolk and Western Railway General Offices, North Building

1 The archives of the Norfolk and Western Railway Company, Roanoke, Va.

Bibliography

Archival Sources

Botetourt County Courthouse, Fincastle, Va.

First Presbyterian Church, Roanoke, Va.

Fishburn Library, Hollins College, Va.

Merchants Association of Roanoke Valley, Roanoke, Va.

Montgomery County Courthouse, Christiansburg, Va.

Norfolk and Western Railway Company, Public Relations Department, Roanoke, Va.

Roanoke City Archives, Municipal Building, Roanoke, Va.

Roanoke City Public Library, Virginia Room, Roanoke, Va.

Roanoke College, Salem, Va.

Roanoke County Courthouse, Salem, Va.

Roanoke Times and World-News library, Roanoke, Va.

Roanoke Valley Historical Society, Roanoke, Va.

Salem Presbyterian Church, Salem, Va.

Virginia Historic Landmarks Commission, Richmond, Va.

Virginia State Library, Richmond, Va.

Other Sources

Andrew Boyd and Co., comp. *Virginia State Business Directory, 1871–72.* Richmond, Va.: Benjamin Bates, Bookseller and Publisher, 1871.

Barnes, Raymond P. *A History of Roanoke.* Radford, Va.: Commonwealth Press, 1968.

Bemiller, Sara Boggs. "Magnifico: Italian Splendor on a Hill in South Roanoke." *Roanoker* 7, no. 1 (October 1980):36–40.

Biddle, Owen. *The Young Carpenter's Assistant.* Philadelphia: McCarty and Davis, 1837.

Bixby, Arthur M. "Area Rail History Set Straight." *Roanoke Times and World News,* Wednesday, June 11, 1980, p. A-8.

Breeding, N. K., Jr., and Dawson, J. W. *Roanoke County Groundwater.* State Water Control Board, Bureau of Water Control Management, Planning Bulletin 301. Richmond, Va.: Commonwealth of Virginia, July 1976.

Bruce, Thomas. *Southwest Virginia and Shenandoah Valley.* Richmond, Va.: J. L. Hill Publishing Co., 1891.

Brunvand, Jan Harold, ed. *The Study of American Folklore: An Introduction.* New York: W. W. Norton Co., 1968.

Chataigne, J. H., comp. *Chataigne's Virginia Gazetteer and Classified Business Directory, 1884–'5.* Richmond, Va.: J. H. Chataigne, 1884.

———. *Chataigne's Virginia Gazetteer and Classified Business Directory, 1893–94.* Richmond, Va.: J. H. Chataigne, 1893.

Cheek, Elizabeth. "Benjamin Deyerle, Builder: 1806–1883." B.A. thesis, Hollins College, 1971.

Clark, Kenneth. *The Gothic Revival.* Rev. ed. London: Constable and Co., 1950.

Collingwood, R. G., and Myres, J. N. L. *Roman Britain and the English Settlements.* 2nd ed. Oxford: Clarendon Press, 1937.

Description of the Album of Virginia; or the Old Dominion, Illustrated. Vol. 1. Richmond, Va.: Enquirer Book and Job Printing Office, 1857.

Dorson, Richard M. *Folklore and Folklife: An Introduction.* Chicago: University of Chicago Press, 1972.

Edgell, G. H. *The American Architecture of To-Day.* New York: Charles Scribner's Sons, 1928.

Edward Beyer. Exhibition catalog, Roanoke City Library and The Roanoke Fine Arts Center, April 7–May 18, 1974.

Eisenberg, William Edward. *The First Hundred Years: Roanoke College, 1842–1942.* Strasburg, Va.: Shenandoah Publishing House, 1942.

"Firemen Are in New Quarters: Department Moves into New House—Description of Fine Building," *Roanoke Times,* Wednesday, February 6, 1907, p. 5.

Fisher, Fred. "Rev. P. M. Lewis, Born a Slave in Virginia, Passes His Eighty-fifth Birthday." *Waterloo* (Iowa) *Courier,* March 8, 1934.

Fitchen, John. *The New World Dutch Barn: A Study of Its Characteristics, Its Structural System, and Its Probable Erection Procedures.* Syracuse, N.Y.: Syracuse University Press, 1968.

"F. J. Chapman, Pioneer Hotel Owner of Past." *Salem Times Register* (Roanoke County centennial edition), May 27, 1938, sec. 5, p. 49.

Glassie, Henry. "A Central Chimney Continental Log House." *Pennsylvania Folk Life* 18, no. 2 (winter 1968–69):32–39.

———. *Folk Housing in Middle Virginia.* Knoxville: University of Tennessee Press, 1975.

———. "Old Barns of Appalachia." *Journal of the Roanoke Valley Historical Society* 9, no. 1 (1973–74):1–13.

———. *Pattern in the Material Folk Culture of the Eastern United States.* Philadelphia: University of Pennsylvania Press, 1968.

————. "The Pennsylvania Barn in the South." *Pennsylvania Folklife* 15, no. 4 (summer 1966):12–25.

————. "The Variation of Concepts within Tradition: Barn Building in Otsego County, New York." *Geoscience and Man* 5 (June 10, 1974):177–235.

Goodwin, Edmund P. "Roanoke's 300th Anniversary." *Roanoke Historical Society Journal* 7, no. 2 (1970):30–36.

Gowans, Alan. *Architecture in New Jersey: A Record of American Civilization.* New Jersey Historical Series, vol. 6. Princeton, N.J.: D. Van Nostrand Co., 1964.

Greif, Martin. *Depression Modern: The Thirties Style in America.* New York: Universe Books, 1975.

Hamlin, Talbot. *Greek Revival Architecture in America.* New York: Dover Publications, 1964.

————. *The American Spirit in Architecture.* The Pageant of America, vol. 13. New Haven, Conn.: Yale University Press, 1926.

Hart, John Fraser, and Mather, Eugene Cotton. "The Character of Tobacco Barns and Their Role in the Tobacco Economy of the U.S." In *Annals of the Association of American Geographers*, 51:274–93. Washington, D.C., September 1961.

Heffelfinger, Grace Pierce. "The I House: An Architectural Form in Rockbridge County, Virginia." M.A. thesis, State University of New York at Oneonta, Cooperstown Graduate Program, 1972.

Hinke, Rev. Wm. J., and Kemper, Charles E., eds. "Moravian Diaries of Travels through Virginia: Diary of the Journey of the First Colony of Single Brethren to North Carolina, Oct. 8–Nov. 17, 1853." *Virginia Magazine of History and Biography* 12, no. 2 (October 1904):134–53, and 12, no. 3 (January 1905):271–81.

————. "Moravian Diaries of Travels through Virginia: Extracts from the Diary of Leonhard Schnell and John Brandmueller of Their Journey to Virginia, Oct. 12–Dec. 12, 1749." *Virginia Magazine of History and Biography* 11, no. 2 (October 1903):113–30.

Hitchcock, Henry-Russell. *American Architectural Books.* Minneapolis: University of Minnesota Press, 1962.

"Hotel Roanoke Celebrates: The Completion of a New $225,000 Addition." *Norfolk and Western Magazine* 9, no. 12 (December 1931):697.

Howe, Henry. *Historical Collections of Virginia.* Charleston, S.C.: Babcock and Co., 1845.

Kain, Richard M. "Stalking Nineteenth-Century Virginia with Sketchbook and Pen." *Colonial Williamsburg Today* 1, no. 4 (summer 1979):6–8.

Kegley, F. B. *Kegley's Virginia Frontier.* Roanoke, Va.: Southwest Virginia Historical Society, 1938.

Kidney, Walter C. *The Architecture of Choice: Eclecticism in America, 1880–1930.* New York: George Braziller, 1974.

Kincanon, Luci Shaw. "Roanoke County Barns of the Nineteenth Century." *Journal of the Roanoke Valley Historical Society* 8, no. 2 (summer 1972):14–26.

Lancaster, Clay. "The American Bungalow." *Art Bulletin* 40, no. 3 (September 1958):239–53.

Lane, Johnathan. "The Period House in the 1920s." *Journal of the Society of Architectural Historians* 20, no. 4 (1961):169–78.

Larkin, Oliver W. *Art and Life in America.* New York: Holt, Rinehart and Winston, 1960.

Lewis, Helen. "What They Owned in the 1840s." *Journal of the Roanoke Valley Historical Society* 10, no. 2 (1978):34–53.

Long, Amos, Jr. "Bakeovens in the Pennslyvania Folk-Culture." *Pennsylvania Folklife* 14, no. 2 (Dec. 1964):16–29.

————. "Outdoor Bakeovens in Berks." *Historical Review of Berks County* 38, no. 1 (winter 1962–63):11–14, 31–32.

Lugar, Norma. "The Tragic Genius of Robert Allen." *Roanoker* 5, no. 1 (Jan.–Feb. 1978):30–33, 60–63.

Lyle, Royster, Jr. "Log Buildings in the Valley of Virginia." *Journal of the Roanoke Historical Society* 8, no. 1 (winter 1972):24–31.

————, and Simpson, Pamela Hemenway. *The Architecture of Historic Lexington.* Charlottesville: University Press of Virginia, 1977.

Maass, John. "Architecture and Americanism: Or Pastiches of Independence Hall." *Historic Preservation* 22, no. 2 (April-June 1970):17–25.

Martin, Joseph. *A New and Comprehensive Gazetteer of Virginia.* Charlottesville, Va.: Joseph Martin, 1836.

McCauley, William, ed. *History of Roanoke County, Salem, Roanoke City, Virginia, and Representative Citizens.* Chicago: Biographical Publishing Co., 1902.

Mercer, Henry C. *The Origin of Log Houses in the United States.* Reprinted from Bucks County Historical Society Papers, vol. 5 (1926), with additions. Doylestown, Pa.: The Bucks County Historical Society, 1967.

Minton, Cronin. "Progress Closing in on Fire Station no. 1," *Roanoke Times*, Sunday, November 1, 1970, p. C-8.

Moorman, J. J., M.D. *Mineral Springs of North America: How to Reach and How to Use Them.* Philadelphia: J. B. Lippincott & Co., 1873.

———. *The Virginia Springs and Springs of the South and West*. Philadelphia: J. B. Lippincott & Co., 1859.

Niederer, Frances J. *Hollins College: An Illustrated History*. Charlottesville, Va.: University Press of Virginia, 1973.

———. *The Town of Fincastle, Virginia*. Charlottesville: University Press of Virginia, 1965.

Norfolk and Western Railway, *Tourists and Excursionists Guide Book: Summer Homes*. Philadelphia: National Bureau of Engraving & Mf'g. Co., 1882.

Pierce, Eleanor G. "Vacations of Yesteryear." *Norfolk and Western Magazine* 15, no. 6 (June 1937):211.

Pollard, Edward A. *The Virginia Tourist: Sketches of the Springs and Mountains of Virginia*. Philadelphia: J. B. Lippincott & Co., 1870.

Pugh, James A., and Stewart, Charles I. "Roanoke City, Virginia." Chapter 4 in *South-West Virginia and the Valley*. Roanoke, Va.: A. D. Smith and Co., 1892.

Rhoads, William B. *The Colonial Revival*. 2 vols. New York: Garland Publishing, 1977.

"Roanoke Architecture." Mimeographed. Hollins, Va.: Hollins College, 1969.

Roanoke, Virginia, Directory: 1913, Roanoke, Va.: Hill Directory Company, Inc., 1913.

Salem, Virginia: Its Advantages and Attractions. New York: The Giles Co. Print, 1891.

Scott, Margaret. "Thomas and Tasker Tosh: The Brothers Who Owned Roanoke." *Journal of the Roanoke Historical Society* 2, no. 1 (summer 1965):5–11.

1776: The British Story of the American Revolution. Exhibition catalog, National Maritime Museum, Greenwich, England, April 14– October 2, 1976, London: Times Books, 1976.

Shurtleff, H. R. *The Log Cabin Myth*. Cambridge, Mass.: Harvard University Press, 1939.

Sloane, Eric. *An Age of Barns*. New York: Ballantine Books, 1975.

———. *American Barns and Covered Bridges*. New York: Funk and Wagnalls, 1954.

Snow, W. H. *Snow's Modern Barn System of Raising and Curing Tobacco*. Baltimore: n.p., 1890.

Stinnett, Julie. "Walter Izard's Map of Roanoke County." M.A. thesis, Hollins College, 1977.

Stoner, Robert Douthat. *A Seed-Bed of the Republic*. Radford, Va.: Commonwealth Press, 1962.

Swaim, Doug, ed. *Carolina Dwelling: The Student Publication of the School of Design*. Vol. 26. Raleigh: North Carolina State University, 1978.

Turner, Robert P., ed. *Lewis Miller: Sketches and Chronicles*. York, Pa.: The Historical Society of York County, 1966.

Virginia Historic Landmarks Commission, The Historic American Buildings Survey, comp. *Virginia Catalog*. Charlottesville, Va.: University Press of Virginia, 1976.

Waller, James O. *Geohydrology of the Upper Roanoke River Basin, Virginia*. Virginia State Water Control Board, Bureau of Water Control Management, Planning Bulletin 302. Richmond, Va.; August 1976.

Walsh, W. H., comp. *Walsh's Roanoke, Virginia, City Directory for 1900*. Charleston, S.C.: W. H. Walsh Directory Co., 1900.

Wayland, John W. *A History of Shenandoah County, Virginia*. Strasburg, Va.: Shenandoah Publishing House, 1927.

Westlager, C. A. *The Log Cabin in America*. New Brunswick, N.J.: Rutgers University Press, 1969.

Whiffen, Marcus. *American Architecture since 1780: A Guide to the Styles*. Cambridge, Mass.: M.I.T. Press, 1969.

Whitwell, W. L. "Saint Andrew's Roman Catholic Church: Roanoke's High Victorian Gothic Landmark." *Virginia Cavalcade* 24, no. 3 (winter 1975):124–33.

———, and Winborne, Lee W. "The Sedon Journal." *Journal of the Roanoke Valley Historical Society* 10, no. 1 (1977):1–27.

Wingfield, Robert F. "Historic and Famous Springs." In "Roanoke County History," p. 3. Manuscript (1942) in W.P.A. vertical file: "Roanoke County Springs," Roanoke City Public Library, Roanoke, Va.

Wise, John S. *The End of an Era*. Boston and New York: Houghton, Mifflin and Co., 1899.

Woodward, Herbert P. *Geology and Mineral Resources of the Roanoke Area, Virginia*. Charlottesville, Va.: State Commission on Conservation and Development, Virginia Geological Survey, University of Virginia, 1932.

Worrell, Anne Lowry, comp. *Over the Mountain Men: Their Early Court Records in Southwest Virginia*. Baltimore: Genealogical Publishing Co., 1962.

Wright, R. Lewis. "Edward Beyer and the Album of Virginia." *Virginia Cavalcade* 22, no. 4 (spring 1973):36–46.

Writers' Program of the Work Projects Administration in the State of Virginia. *Roanoke: Story of City and County*. Roanoke: Stone Printing and Manufacturing Company, 1942.

Index

Italic indicates page numbers of illustrations.